# MERLIN'S HANDBOOK
## FOR SEEKERS AND STARSEEDS

# MERLIN'S HANDBOOK
## FOR SEEKERS AND STARSEEDS

A Guide to Awakening Your Divine Potential

Margaret Doner

iUniverse LLC
Bloomington

**MERLIN'S HANDBOOK FOR SEEKERS AND STARSEEDS**
A Guide to Awakening Your Divine Potential

Copyright © 2013 Margaret Doner.

All rights reserved. No part of this book may be used or reproduced by any means, graphic, electronic, or mechanical, including photocopying, recording, taping or by any information storage retrieval system without the written permission of the publisher except in the case of brief quotations embodied in critical articles and reviews.

iUniverse books may be ordered through booksellers or by contacting:

iUniverse LLC
1663 Liberty Drive
Bloomington, IN 47403
www.iuniverse.com
1-800-Authors (1-800-288-4677)

Because of the dynamic nature of the Internet, any web addresses or links contained in this book may have changed since publication and may no longer be valid. The views expressed in this work are solely those of the author and do not necessarily reflect the views of the publisher, and the publisher hereby disclaims any responsibility for them.

Any people depicted in stock imagery provided by Thinkstock are models, and such images are being used for illustrative purposes only. Certain stock imagery © Thinkstock.

ISBN: 978-1-4917-1711-0 (sc)
ISBN: 978-1-4917-1713-4 (hc)
ISBN: 978-1-4917-1712-7 (e)

Printed in the United States of America.

iUniverse rev. date: 12/12/2013

# Table of Contents

Acknowlegments ............................................................................... vii
Introduction ........................................................................................ ix

| | | |
|---|---|---|
| Chapter One | Waking Up .................................................................. 1 | |
| Chapter Two | The Journey On Earth ............................................. 16 | |
| Chapter Three | Know Thyself: Integration Of The Soul ............. 30 | |
| Chapter Four | Collaborating With The Angelic Realm ............. 36 | |
| Chapter Five | Creation On And Off Earth ................................... 43 | |
| Chapter Six | The Attack Of The Dark .......................................... 53 | |
| Chapter Seven | The Fall From Eden—Karmic Imprints Of The Starseeds ............................................................. 65 | |
| Chapter Eight | Soul Contracts And How To Break (Or Honor) Them ..................................................... 94 | |
| Chapter Nine | Nephilim, Angels, Dragons And Reptilians ................................................................... 106 | |
| Chapter Ten | Sacred Tools And Symbols— Their Use And Misuse ............................................ 117 | |
| Chapter Eleven | Death And Dying .................................................... 132 | |
| Chapter Twelve | Knowledge, Truth And Freedom ........................ 140 | |
| Chapter Thirteen | Manifesting Your Gifts: This And More Shall Ye Do ................................. 145 | |

# Acknowlegments

This book is dedicated to all the Seekers and Starseeds who have been in my life over the twenty-plus years I've been doing this work. Your collective stories are contained in these pages. This book is for you.

# Introduction

This Handbook is a collaborative effort between me, Merlin, and the many people who have come to see me for angelic channeling and past life regression therapy over the years. As my clients have been awakening, so too have I awoken; and as I have awoken, so too have my clients. This is my sixth spiritual book and those of you who have followed the path of my writing will know, because they are truly my inspiration, where my clients have been going by reading the books I have written. It is my belief that life provides us all the opportunity to learn and grow through the experiences we encounter and that when we are encouraged to share, rather than suppress, we all benefit. My experience has been that when people do not fear they will be judged they share enormous amounts of information that appears to others to be outside the norm.

The suppression of metaphysical information has marginalized some ideas and experiences and made many people think they were going crazy when something happened to them that appeared to be "outside the box." For many of us the veil between dimensions is thinning, and metaphysical experiences once deemed insane are now being accepted and even in some cases understood. People see ghosts, angels, demons, and ETs. People astral travel, and step off the lower matrix. They also remember past lives and even lives on other planets or in other dimensions. People access their lives between lives and integrate who they are in deeper and deeper ways. Our challenge is to step into mastery with these experiences and not into fear. In other lives we would have been called witches and demons and burned at the stake or sent away from the village by fearful people. Today the challenge is to listen and sit side-by-side with this information and integrate it into our consciousness without pushing it away or believing it unconditionally. We must discern. We must not be afraid. We must be open-minded, gentle, loving and kind to those who wish to speak of things that frighten us.

It doesn't mean that angels, extra-terrestrials, demons and other non-physical beings are not controversial topics for discussion. Everyone has an opinion about these and in a scientific-based culture, such as the United States, it can be difficult to find someone with whom to discuss such things—even today. And yet, supernatural television shows, and movies are everywhere. So, clearly we are fascinated and even science cannot stop the truth of thousands of people's personal experiences with unseen paranormal energies. Whether demonic or angelic, first-hand experiences with these beings are being documented as we seek to understand our position in this multidimensional universe.

The purpose of this handbook is to assist you, step-by-step, to release fear and reclaim your mastery. As you move through the chapters Merlin stimulates you to consider such things as: self-awareness, karmic imprints, reclaiming your galactic identity, and recognizing, identifying and collaborating with non-physical energies. Use this handbook as a guide. It does not take you by the hand and tell you what to think; rather it suggests exercises to expand your awareness so that you can come to your own conclusions. I share with you both my and other people's experiences through the pages of this book. My personal search for truth has led me to many interesting places, some of which are recorded here.

Merlin respects a Seeker who truly seeks, and that means you assume you don't know it yet, and you don't censor. I have found that this approach has allowed me to accept and process a myriad of experiences, both personal and those which have been reported by my clients, without judgment, and even more importantly, without fear.

This book is not about giving away our power to anyone, or anything, and that includes angels, Merlin, gurus, priests or friends. It is about learning to trust ourselves, our hearts, our intuition, and our common sense. It is about growing up and taking responsibility for our choices, as individuals and a collective. It is about learning to love more deeply and awakening compassion for ourselves and others. We live in a world of duality, both night and day exist, and it is time to live in balance with both dark and light once again, and stop the relentless battle, both inside and outside ourselves. The battle of dark and light benefits no one. God is big enough for All That Is; God is big enough for all of us.

So, grab a journal to record your adventures and start your journey of self-exploration. Each chapter has an exercise at the end to anchor what you have just read and to help you to integrate the information. Merlin and I thank you for joining us, and remember: You are always where you are meant to be.

# Chapter One

## *Waking Up*

*Love does not delight in evil, but rejoices with the truth.*
*1 Corinthians 13*

Many people are experiencing a profound awakening. They are taking a journey of self-awareness that includes the integration of their previous lives, the knowledge of their higher or divine self, the ability to work in conscious alignment with their spiritual guides and Higher Self, and the release of fear. Why is this happening to so many? What force is bringing this experience of awakening to so many people worldwide? What is the purpose behind it? Are we involved in some type of collective consciousness that links us all together and urges us to obtain greater and greater states of awareness? As a species are we being urged to move from young soul consciousness to maturity? Is it merely happenstance, or is a purpose or power urging us along? Are we, in fact, being collectively "pushed from the nest" and challenged to fly for our own survival?

Leading this awakening is a group of people often dubbed Starseeds and Seekers. The names in many ways are interchangeable. All Seekers are Starseeds, but not all Starseeds are Seekers. As a knowledge-gatherer, a Seeker is fascinated with life, and life creation, and in their quest to understand other life forms they will incarnate throughout the many galaxies. During these incarnations they will take on many different bodies and forms of creation.

A Starseed is defined as someone who has incarnated on other planets besides the Earth, but is not necessarily a Seeker studying life creation. The common bond they share is a knowing that they have lived on other worlds besides the Earth, and a desire to awaken and remember those other incarnations. Many of these people are at the forefront of the revolution to awaken human consciousness from the lower matrix that ensnares us and keeps us captive through our ego.

I believe at the heart of this self-awareness work is the desire to reclaim the gifts many of us had long ago on other planets (and in some cases also on Earth). These gifts include mental telepathy, telekinesis, and teleportation, among others. Although to some this might sound like science fiction, the ability to use what are dubbed "paranormal gifts" is recorded in many books. *The PK Man* by Jeffrey Mishlove is one such book. It is a fascinating exploration of a man, named Ted Owens, who had a phenomenal gift to control weather and earthquakes with his psychokinetic abilities. Ted Owens and his magical powers bring us smack dab into the topic of right use of will, and the misuse of these gifts throughout time. Those of us who believe that gifts such as psychokinetic powers are possible, also recognize that this power is *only* to be awoken with right intention and love. For many Starseeds, the desire is not only to awaken these gifts, but to use them in alignment with the right use of will. This is why I believe I have witnessed so many people remembering not only their past lives on the planet Earth, but lives on other planets as well. They have memories of a time on other planets when they could perform magic. They lived in harmony with nature, and shared true community without the push and pull of ego.

*(Another book which details this type of phenomenon is: China's Super Psychics, by Paul Dong and Thomas E. Raffill, and China's Major Mysteries, also by Paul Dong. These books detail the abilities of China's psychic children. They beg the question: "How will we use these gifts when they awaken?")*

People who identify with the Starseed moniker often remember when they incarnated onto the Earth with these gifts, and they were punished for them, burned at the stake or tortured. They were called witches and feared for their knowledge. Most of the time the knowledge was simple; it was the knowledge of herbs and how to use them for medicinal purposes, but I have also witnessed people remembering lives on the Earth when they could do miraculous things; create orb balls in their hands, release electricity from their fingertips, and utilize the power of crystals in alignment with their own consciousness. During the time of Atlantis these gifts were in wide use. However, the ego-mind was not tamed, and wizards of all types grew drunk with the power they had over others by misusing their gifts. Wizard Wars were common as wizards used their power against one another, and became masters of mind control and black magic. Clearly, this was not an expression of the right use of will.

*(A wizard skill, remote viewing, is taught by David Morehouse. David was trained by the CIA, and clearly speaks about the gifts, and dangers, associated with this skill. If you are interested in reading more about this you can pick up his book, Remote Viewing: The Complete User's Manual for Coordinate Remote Viewing.)*

The people who remember these experiences often remember lives on other planets during a time when intergalactic war was raging. They have memories of their peaceful communities being invaded by aggressive species that took away their freedom, and shut down their gifts. Some of these invaders were Reptilian, some spider-like, some robots, but they all had one intention: to destroy these innocent civilizations, and take control of their planet. These wars are called the Orion Wars and I write about their origin in my book entitled, *Merlin's War: The Battle between the Family of Light and the Family of Dark*.

The Orion War karma is all around us today. It is in our movies (*Harry Potter series, Avatar, Lord of the Rings, Star Wars, Enders Game* to name a few), it is in our television programs (*Star Trek, Battlestar Galactica* and too numerous to mention). It is in our personal relationships, and our history. The destruction of the Native American cultures is parallel to the Orion War stories that took place on other planets. Whether you believe that karma comes back, or history repeats itself, it is my contention that we are currently smack dab in the middle of the Orion Wars and most of us don't know it. There is a battle on for control of the planet Earth, and most of us know this (or feel it) but we don't understand it. We don't understand the key players, we don't understand their intention, and we don't know what role we play in their drama for world domination.

Many contend that waking up means no longer allowing ourselves to be manipulated by what some have dubbed, "The Powers that Be." Others believe that it is bad for us to pay attention to the world news and events because it brings us down. Those who believe that we must uncover the darkness to liberate ourselves from it often butt heads with those who believe that we should protect our vibrational fields by looking the other way. It appears that few can agree on *how* to get our power back, but many will agree that they want just that. They want to be liberated and safe, and although they agree on the end goal, they may disagree on how to achieve it.

During the 1930's and 1940's when Hitler was waging a war that began in Europe, and soon became worldwide, it was easy to see the plan. The plan was to destroy inferior species and build an ideal world for those you deem worthy. This is identical to the Reptilian intergalactic agenda which is the desire to destroy inferior species and maintain superiority. Some believe that the ability to perform DNA manipulation and cloning comes directly from extraterrestrial technology, and many people contend that Hitler and his top aides were closely involved with extra-terrestrials and attempting to replicate their technology. After WWII the United States hired the Nazi scientists and engineers (dubbed *Project Paperclip*), and paid them to continue their work here, which they did primarily in the military bases around America.

*(The disagreement of how to keep ourselves safe is not a new one. I recently talked with a ninety-year-old German-Jewish woman whose mother was ridiculed and poo-pooed for trying to awaken her relatives to the dangers of Hitler. Fortunately for her, her father finally listened and the family escaped just in time.)*

Currently many of us are concerned about the state of our food, water and air. We have come to understand that the food is toxic to our health because of pesticides, GMOs, hydrogenated fats, high fructose corn syrup and the like. We have read about Monsanto and their worldwide attack on food production, as they seek to own the patents on all the seeds, and make it nearly impossible for organic growers. Once we awaken we don't merely say, "Oh, well we just have to pick and scrounge to find good food," instead we say, "It points to deep sickness in our world that we must be at war with our food supply, and much of our food is becoming toxic to our health."

As we begin to awaken we no longer take for granted the state of our water, our air, our food, and the manner in which we live, and we understand that all of this is currently designed not for optimal living enjoyment for all, but for the enjoyment of those at the top of the pyramid, while the majority of the world's population suffers with disease, torture and fascism. The "Occupy" movement coined the phrase the 99% and the 1%. How strange, we think, that so much awakening is taking place amidst so much darkness. The dolphins and whales are being killed with sonar. The polar bears are losing their habitat, and according to Michael Kelley of the *Business Insider*, "Ecuador is planning to auction off three million of the country's 8.1 million hectares of pristine Amazonian rainforest to Chinese oil companies." He also reports that this is happening at the same time that Peru declared an environmental state of emergency in its northern Amazon rainforest. Besides the environmental issues, those of us who followed the loss of personal freedom since the Patriot Act (and beyond) realize that our rights are being curtailed, and we are being watched at every moment as cameras record your every move in many of the large cities. How incongruous it seems.

So many people ask, "What is the purpose of life?" Is it what some believe: To awaken mankind to a better way of living? Is it merely to exist and grow, each at our own pace? Is it for us to learn and suffer the karmic consequences of so much war being waged? Why have the Starseeds (those with memories from lives on other planets) come to the Earth and brought their gifts, awakening, and karma with them?

I believe the time has come for us to reawaken our Starseed gifts even more fully, but this time with the right use of will. Jesus told us what path we are to take when, after performing one of his miracles, he said: "This too and more shall ye do." As divine beings we know how to perform "magic."

Why then do we take these journeys to purify the ego, release ourselves from fear, and put ourselves into right relationship with others? I believe it is because we know that at this time only those who have done all those things can be trusted to hold these old "Atlantean" powers without the powers falling into misuse, and repeating the ancient Wizard Wars. We are now aware of karmic payback and realize that what we "sow we reap."

If we awaken from our sleep of innocence we will be quite different from the extraterrestrials we were long ago (Pleiadians, Lyrians, Regulans, Arcturians, Sirians etc . . .) when we were first attacked on our home planets and our gifts taken from us. We are now Mature and Old Souls who have learned the hard way, and can hold our gifts with wisdom. We have seen both the Dark and the Light, and we understand how both sides operate. We have begun to re-empower ourselves with our own personal truths. Mastery, we realize, means holding the truth of all things without fear; it means that as we awaken and utilize our gifts, we also look in the mirror and tame our egos.

As we reconnect to our divinity, and begin to awaken these gifts, those who wish to keep us in fear, and disempowered, will not welcome this perceived challenge to their power. If we can teleport we no longer need cars or oil companies. If we can hold orbs of energy in our hands we can keep ourselves warm. If we can manifest food in the palms of our hands we can free ourselves from Monsanto and pesticides. Perhaps the generation called the Indigo and Crystal children were meant to hold these gifts and have been (as some believe) targeted by vaccines and cell tower (and other) frequencies to keep their gifts at bay. Perhaps if their noses are kept in laptops, and their fingers busy texting, they will not be free to manifest their true powers. Diversions are everywhere, and many people are frightened of silence. Let us begin to awaken these wizard powers with the vibration of love intact in our hearts, and truly free ourselves, at last, from the dark agenda of fear that tries to keep us enslaved. Let us become the Co-Creator Gods we always have been. This book is my, and Merlin's, intention to assist that awakening. It is through this awakening that we reclaim our mastery and learn to trust ourselves once again.

As we move from being innocents into true awakening we realize that it is not the job of someone else to build our Merkabah (or carriage for our soul), it is our job to reawaken this vehicle. It is not the responsibility of someone else to hold the Light for us, or keep us safe; it is our responsibility to become fully-realized adult souls. It is our job to stop acting like children who need others to tell us what to think or believe. We realize that we no longer will give up our power to others who we deem better, but humbly begin the journey to reunite with our inner truth, and the divine heart within us. Teachers should release us into the world, not keep us tethered to them like children. This is true empowerment, and it is essential that we do not continue to give away our power to others, but learn to trust our intuition and allow the mastery to evolve as a natural expression of the healing process of our own wounding.

The awakening is in stages. An important part of the journey must include reconnecting to the original wounding so that we understand it, and it no longer holds us in its sway. This is the moment that we fell out of the "Garden of Eden." As you will see in Chapter Seven, those memories will clarify for you the template of your subsequent lives, and the fears and motivations that hold you in their sway even today. Your trigger buttons are often a reflection of those stories. Also required is releasing the fears that keep you small. Are you afraid of being different? Are you afraid of being seen, and harmed for your gifts? Are you afraid of harming others? Are you afraid of others not approving of you, or liking you? These questions must be answered and healed. Once the fear has been cleansed, the right use of will must be firmly anchored. Only then will these miraculous gifts (given originally to liberate us) be re-awoken. And finally, we must learn to trust the gifts and our ability to use them with love and wisdom; once we understand that there are karmic consequences to the actions we make, we are very careful about what we do.

As we awaken to the idea of a multi-dimensional reality, we also begin to comprehend that dimensions are not a place, but a state of consciousness. The angels exist in a higher dimension because they exist in a higher state of consciousness. Humans exist in a lower dimensional realm because they are dense and solid, and so they exist in a lower consciousness realm.

If you are eager to understand what role Merlin plays in all of this, and what his Seeker school is all about, you will enjoy this book. It is a guide to understanding how this might be achieved.

## WHO IS MERLIN AND WHAT IS A SEEKER?

For most people the name Merlin evokes images of wizards and warlocks, and a time when Dragons and fair maidens roamed the Earth. There is scarcely a human (at least one coached in the Western European traditions) who hasn't heard of Camelot, Arthur, Guinevere, Lancelot, and Merlin. Books, movies, television shows, and monuments trumpet their existence. They are as much a part of our collective consciousness as Moses parting the Red Sea, and equally debated as to whether the stories are fable or fact-filled. Modern man has clamped down his mind to the possibility of magic and has relegated it to a Disneyland status. Seekers know that magic is holy.

Seekers travel throughout time and space to fearlessly seek truth. What binds them together is the willingness to go anywhere to understand something that previously eluded them. Neither shadow nor light frightens them. Earth-bound Seekers use this planet as their classroom. Seekers understand that their human ego, while at times useful, at other times is a hindrance. The human ego will settle for mediocrity. The human ego will convince the Seeker that he or she is intellectually superior, or that what they seek to understand is unknowable. The human ego will defend a point of view rather than listen patiently. All of this is counterproductive to the Seeker of Truth.

Earth gives a Seeker something beyond the scope of any other planetary system: amazing variety. During their many incarnations upon Earth humans will be kings and paupers, orphans and fat, happy children, perpetrators and victims, and all of these experiences make them wiser and more knowledgeable. All of these experiences keep the ego flexible. At times they will be drawn to spiritual communities thinking that they will be taught humility, or perhaps gain a clearer perspective on God.

If you are a Seeker you have chosen a difficult, but rewarding, path. The more you learn, the more you evolve, the harder the lessons become; but the more "tools" you have in your toolbox. You may wonder why Seekers and Merlin are joined together in this book. It is because every true Seeker longs to understand the greatest mystery and gift of all: life creation. Who better than the Master Wizard himself to teach a Seeker how to do magic? When Merlin uses magic it is not a trick; it is the holy expression of God's energy used in balance to create life. On Earth holy men sit with sinners, providing a banquet table of rich experiences. On Earth the holy man and the sinner within us is also ever present, as we recognize that what is outside of us is also within.

Seekers understand that turning water into wine is divine magic. Modern man explains his existence through either a biblical explanation such as "God did it," or a scientific one, "Evolutionary natural forces did it," but neither one satisfies the ancient craving to be a part of creation. Seekers see it differently. A Seeker remembers times and places that fairy books have forgotten, and Seekers know that skyscrapers (although wondrous in many ways) do not teach them the rich lessons held in nature. They also believe that although man was meant to be a creational being, that creation can turn to destruction when the ego is given free reign. They also know that earning the right to be a Creator God is a sacred one. True Seekers seek not to challenge God and natural law, but to live harmoniously within it—a part of All That Is. True magic is not wishful thinking. True magic *is* God. True magic is sacred wisdom. Sacred wisdom is the truth each and every one of us carries deep within our soul. We have always been given free will; the will to create reality with our minds. We have been given free will to create and use our opposable thumbs to see our creations manifest.

The Seeker School is Merlin's school of Creational Truth. Merlin is a teacher above all else; he is a teacher longing to bring his students into conscious mastery and alignment with Universal Law and Truth. Merlin understands that if human beings do not wake up and begin to create in alignment with Universal Law, once again creation will become destruction.

If you are struggling to accept that the act of creation has been put in the hands of mere mortals, consider this: every living and breathing thing is a creator in their own right. Ants create ant colonies, bees create hives and honey, birds create nests of all shapes and sizes, and all creatures reproduce as the ultimate expression of creation. Each of us creates as an expression of our basic nature. If we accept the fact that the urge to create was given to all living things from God, then it isn't difficult to imagine that the need to create is not limited to life on Earth, but extends throughout the Multiverse as a universal expression of God. The urge to create, destroy, and re-create again, is a natural expression of the Source of All.

As a soul evolves into greater states of higher awareness and consciousness, so too does their need to express themselves in more expansive ways. If you believe in the one-life theory, I ask you to suspend your current belief system enough to imagine that the path of evolution a soul takes occurs both when incarnate on the third-dimensional Earth, but also when disincarnate as well. In other words, when you die to the third-dimensional Earth plane, and cease to reincarnate upon the Earth, it doesn't mean that you die. It merely means that you continue your evolutionary path as a Transcendental Soul. This means you are now a soul ready for even greater lessons; and also greater responsibilities as a Co-Creator God.

Merlin is a Creator God, or what some call an Ascended Master. That means that he has attained a level in his evolutionary path where he has learned how to manipulate energy into form and create life from it. He is an alchemist. He has reincarnated upon the Earth many times, not only as the wizard known as Merlin. As a Creator God his most important creation is the human template. This template is not exclusive to Earth, but has been reproduced with various modifications throughout the Multiverse. The students in Merlin's Transcendental Seeker School are learning to become alchemists and eventually, perhaps, Creator Gods themselves; learning to bring principles of sacred geometry into form in alignment with the right use of will. They have evolved enough that they are ready to take all the wisdom they have gathered while incarnating throughout time and space and apply it to life creation. Some of these Seeker' students have come to Earth with their gifts intact, as previously mentioned, but how they apply them while on the planet is dictated by their free-will.

The students in Merlin's school must have passed many strict tests. They must have integrity, honesty, and practice unconditional love. They must understand karma, humility, and trust in the God Consciousness. In the Transcendental Seeker School the student deepens their understanding of natural laws, and learns how to create life forms in harmony with these laws. Unlike many scientists on Earth, who are still young souls and have not understood fully the ramifications of their actions, the students in Merlin's Transcendental Seeker School are bound to a very strict code of ethics.

On Earth the ego wrestles with the Higher Self. The human ego battles with the egoless Higher Self for survival. The ego feels that the Higher Mind is its enemy, and will continually struggle against the Higher Mind. For example, the Higher Self will be patient and allow a situation to unfold with faith, while the ego will strike out and demand instant gratification. Even after they have graduated from their Earthly incarnations, and have begun their work in Merlin's Transcendental Seeker School, a Seeker who finds they struggle with control issues and has difficulty allowing their creations to evolve without constant tinkering, might have to reincarnate upon the Earth once again. While incarnated they will struggle with impatience, which gives them the opportunity to re-learn patience. The witnessing of how impatience can bring disaster will be reinforced on Earth in ways that it can't be in other dimensional realms, and the student will be sharply reminded of the need to release their strict control over their creation, and over-see, but not dominate, that which they have birthed.

There have been a number of famous Transcendental Soul Age Seekers who have incarnated on the Earth to assist others, and I view Mahatma Gandhi as one of these. Obviously, he had imperfections because he was human, but he also had the ability to find God in the darkness.

Merlin guides and teaches the Seekers whose ultimate goal is to be a life creator themselves. Creator Gods are those who create planets, and worlds, with the assistance of other Creator Gods. Merlin is a Creator God and he is responsible for overseeing Earth. That is why his students use Earth as a school room; it is a very difficult school, but as you can imagine, if you are going to be given the ultimate responsibility to create life forms you will need to be taught not only what works but what doesn't! Earth's extremes provide an often harsh, but effective, schoolroom.

Not every person who incarnates on Earth is going to graduate from the Earthly plane, and automatically become a Seeker; but those who choose to be Seekers will always be required to incarnate upon the Earth, and complete the human soul cycle. The human soul cycle consists of Infant, Baby, Young, Mature and Old Soul incarnations. Each stage can have many, many incarnations within it. Some souls will take hundreds or even in some cases thousands of lives to complete the full cycle.

Discernment is one of the most difficult and sophisticated lessons a soul learns. It is essential for an evolved soul to learn discernment and how to "feel" truth. Younger souls are more easily duped, and more likely to fall for charlatans who offer to "save them." Older and Mature Souls may want to be trusting, but they will learn far more quickly who they can and can't trust with their heart. They are also far more aware that they must "save themselves."

Whereas the ego will accuse someone of being evil, or exalt them into the position of being pure good, the Higher Mind will sit alongside others with patience and unattached good will because the Higher Self is neutral. The desire to see everyone as good or well-meaning, or evil and diabolical, can trip up even the more advanced soul until they realize that discernment is necessary for self-protection, and that paranoia can result from fear-based thinking. In his school Merlin stresses the notion that, "What one *wants* to be true, and what *is* true, are not the same thing." Mastery requires a great deal of neutrality when considering others; judgment results not in condemnation, but understanding.

Often teachers from the Seeker School will assist younger Seekers who are still completing their Earthly incarnations. These teachers will either come to Earth as "walk-ins," meaning that they will enter, not through the birth canal, but by taking a human body that was scheduled for death; or they will appear and disappear to aid and assist in the form of an angel, or spirit guide. An evolved Earth Seeker will not require such a profound intervention as a physical appearance by their guide; their guide can reach them by merely providing subtle energy shifts. Earth is a difficult place to incarnate, even for more highly evolved beings. The challenges are ever present and the creation of difficult karma, although an excellent teaching tool, can trip up a soul for many lifetimes as they endlessly repeat their lessons.

These days Merlin is a very strict teacher and he does not mince words or molly-coddle. His student, known to humans as Vlad Dracula, taught him quite early on not to allow any student to continue in his school if they exhibit arrogance and egotism that cannot be tamed. It is hard for humans to imagine that Creator Gods are learning and evolving too, but they are. Like all beings they too are evolving over millions and millions of years. Over the many millennia they too have grown in wisdom. Truly it is: "As above, so below." We are all a part of the same cosmic soup.

Merlin feels that if humankind is to learn from their (and his) mistakes, he needs to make some of what he understands available to humanity. That is why he has urged me to write this Handbook. I have been working with the Archangels and Merlin for many years; I have been channeling them, and teaching others to access them as guides, and channel them as well. I have also recorded and listened to the memories of my clients. These memories have included fantastic other-worldly experiences, as well as alien abductions. My desire to sit with neutrality and allow these memories to unfold for people, I believe, assists them to heal these stories and integrate and move past them. Recovering memories has taken my clients through many dimensions, into afterlife experiences, and into their previous lives.

At the end of each chapter are exercises to assist the reader to anchor some of the ideas presented in the chapter. Written below is an example of the initiation pledge taken by each student in Merlin's school. The heart-center is referenced not because it refers to the actual heart as an organ, but because it represents the soul. Pledging your heart in the spirit realm is the same as pledging your God-Self and is considered sacred. Interestingly enough, in a human the strongest electromagnetic frequencies emanate from the heart. The electrical field as measured in an electrocardiogram is about sixty times greater in amplitude than the brain waves recorded in an electroencephalogram! Here lies the secret to manifestation: the gifts are awoken through the heart, not the mind. The heart is the true power center.

Although the pledge may seem strict to us earthlings, it is absolutely necessary because of the enormous responsibility bestowed upon the students. In the beginning, Merlin did not require this pledge. The pledge is not a binding contract and free will is still honored. Yet, Merlin wants each student to understand that if they are to work with him he has certain expectations. If you choose not to uphold those it is certainly your right. It is also *his* right to decide whether or not to continue working with you if you do not uphold the ideas in the pledge. He does not punish you, but he is very truthful in declaring his point of view on everything.

In the beginning, enrollment in Merlin's school was lax. Students more or less came and went as they pleased, and enjoyed the freedom to play with energy, and create life without restriction. After Merlin's war with Dracula (the idea that Dracula is actually the being we know as Satan will be discussed later) he came to understand the sacred nature of what he was teaching and how it could go awry; as a result this initiation pledge was created. The pledge *is not* intended to be your pledge; after reading this pledge you will be guided to write *your own* pledge to yourself: A pledge for your own life.

## SEEKERS PLEDGE

I _____ faithfully agree to execute each and every condition stated below. I agree to give my entire heart-centered Self in service to the Seeker School, and God, and I understand that if I choose to drop out of school at any time my re-entry is not guaranteed. It is my understanding that the honors bestowed upon me as a result of my acceptance into this school are not guaranteed as well, and I may be expelled from the school, and those honors withdrawn at any time. It is Merlin's right and privilege to decide if I shall continue in the school and the manner in which I will continue. I agree to any and all terms of schooling that Merlin sees fit, including, but not exclusive to the manner and rate at I progress, and the level which I attain.

I understand that admission into the Seeker School bestows upon me the honor of studying life creation, alchemy, and manifestation, and is a sacred honor which aligns me with God's Will and Natural Law. If I break these Natural Laws at any time while in Seeker School, I will be reassigned to the Earth plane to relearn the law (or laws) I have broken, and will agree to continue reincarnating upon the Earth until the lesson has been relearned. Any failure to relearn the lesson, or adhere to this requirement, is automatic expulsion from Seeker School.

These sacred covenants are known to me, and it is through these that I shall learn the teachings of Merlin's Seeker School. In alignment with All That Is I accept these conditions and terms with:

   a. Love
   b. Forgiveness
   c. Truth
   d. Integrity
   e. Honor
   f. Balance
   g. Wisdom
   h. Knowledge
   i. Passion in my heart.

   _____(your signature)
   _____(Merlin's signature)

**EXERCISE ONE**: This is not intended to be *your* pledge, but an example of a pledge you will make to your Higher Self. Begin your Seeker/Starseed journal and record the information you acquire as you work your way through the exercises in this book. Begin by writing a pledge to yourself, for your own life.

# Chapter Two

## *The Journey On Earth*

Let me begin by clarifying the reincarnation stages on the Earth. It is important to make clear that these stages refer to the *Earthly* human reincarnation cycle; a soul may have done lives on other planets prior to incarnating on the Earth. Of course, like everything else, these are generalizations, but in order to understand a person's motivation, it can be helpful to take a closer look. It will assist you to be soul-age appropriate when dealing with people. A Baby Soul and an Old Soul are very different; just like a baby and a mature man are. You do not treat a toddler like an adult.

Being an Infant Soul does not mean that you were just created from the God Source, it merely means that you have begun your *Earthly* journey. The human soul cycle consists of five stages: Infant, Baby, Young, Mature, and Old Soul. Within each stage are lessons that are appropriate to the soul's age. The best way to approach the understanding of this is to see it as parallel to one human life. Just as the infant child is innocent, and still has a strong connection to the spiritual realms, the Infant Soul arrives on Earth as an innocent. Because they are new to the territory, it is beneficial for an Infant Soul to be born in a smaller community or tribe that is less sophisticated. A large city with a myriad of rules, and constant stimulation, would overwhelm an Infant Soul. A caring and close-knit community is ideal for the Infant Soul to get used to being in a physical body and learn the ropes. An Infant Soul is most likely to be superstitious as they will have a strong sense of the energies that are alive behind the veil, but will not have the sophistication to interpret their experience as they interact with these ghostly beings.

A Baby Soul is like a toddler: self-centered and naïve, but with a strong yearning to branch out and try new things. A Baby Soul is metaphorically learning to walk and talk for the first time, and because the ego develops during this stage they need to satisfy their own pleasure-centers. A great deal of karma is created by the Baby Soul in pursuit of his or her own desires. If a Baby Soul rises to power they will most often be inclined to force others to their own will, but they will not have the cleverness to manipulate the populace as a Young Soul dictator might. They will be heavy-handed in their justice and see fairness as "an eye for an eye," without mercy. Compassion is not a part of their wisdom; you might think of a toddler who wants a toy even when another child in the nursery school has it. The toddler will take the toy, use it for their amusement, and often won't understand why the child they took it from is crying. Being able to relate to another person, and "do unto others as you would have them do unto you," is a more refined consciousness. With religion, the Baby Soul will be very drawn to organized institutions of any faith, but particularly ones with strong guidelines, moral codes, and explanations on how to live that make personal decision making unnecessary.

The Young Soul is most like a teenager, or someone in their twenties. Especially in the middle part of the soul age, they want whatever the world has to offer; and they often want the best and most of it. Early in the young soul age they will often be more timid, and follow blindly the advice of authority. But, that often wears off as the soul gains confidence, and matures. Once the young soul gets a taste of independence, they often charge forth, thinking (just like a teenager) that they have all they need to conquer the world. When this happens patience is not their virtue, and they want what they want, and they want it now. Often what they want is lots of real estate, power, money, and good looks. They are often the trend-setters, looking to be near "the beautiful people." Try to tell a teenager that they don't know it all, and that they will have a very different view on life in the future—that idea goes over like a lead balloon. It is the same with a mid-level Young Soul; they know everything, and everyone else just can't see it.

When a Young Soul has political aspirations their motivation will most often be the prestige, money and power such a position brings. Their ideology will be firmly rooted and, because they know everything, it is unlikely to change. A Young Soul will have the worldliness to rise in business, and often they are drawn to mainstream careers or careers in large corporations. Law enforcement also appeals to the young soul. In religion the Young Soul will still enjoy a church setting, but will be more likely to choose one that offers a more sophisticated interpretation of scripture. Young souls in the late stages (just before they enter the Mature Soul cycle) begin to grasp and implement the ideas of community, compassion, and caring. At that point in the young soul's age, when all that striving begins to sour, they often look for other ways to interact with people.

Mature Souls are equivalent to mature adults. They have the ability to reflect backward and suddenly admit that maybe they don't know everything, and they made mistakes. Mature Souls are more likely to think for themselves, be independent, and be interested in self-expression. Mature Souls make excellent teachers, artists, nurses, doctors, and spiritual seekers. Mature Souls' lives can be very tumultuous as they are involved in heavy karmic clean-up. Mature souls have begun to search inward and are looking for their soul's purpose; they want meaning in their life, and they will travel the world seeking truth. They want a soul mate, not just a marriage partner. They fight for true justice, civil rights, and a better world. Mature souls, like mature adults, still have enough energy and idealism left to impact the world, and the wisdom and patience to understand how to effect change. They are likely to work in non-profit organizations, or as social workers and counselors.

Old Souls realize that the struggles on the Earth are often out of their control, and the idealism of the earlier soul ages can often turn to despair before the Old Soul finally finds peace in resignation. Just like an old person begins to realize that they can only change themselves, the Old Soul begins to realize that self-karma is the focus of this Soul Age. The Old Soul learns that they must love and accept themselves before they can truly help the world. The Old Soul can be a curmudgeon, and want to withdraw from the world much like an old man or woman might want to be a hermit before they die. But, the Old Soul, just like the old person, becomes more and more dependent on others to care for them until they realize the true inter-connectedness of all life, and how dependent we are on one another. The Old Soul sees Spirit in everything and finally understands that religion is everywhere and nowhere, and that God is found not only within four walls, but within all of life. Having been through the mill the Old Soul has a great deal of compassion for others, and knows that nothing is without a price to pay.

It is important to note that each Soul Age will take many, many lifetimes to complete, and that when one is doing one's first life in the Soul Age one will appear much like the previous Soul Age; and when one is doing one's last life in a Soul Age one will appear much like the next soul age. For example, in your first life as a Mature Soul you will have many Young Soul characteristics, while your last life as a Mature Soul will be more like that of an Old Soul. So, after you have completed the full cycle—Infant through Old—you are ready to begin your learning as a Transcendental Soul, or a soul who no longer has to incarnate on the Earth. Once you have begun your Transcendental Soul learning, you are ready to enter Merlin's School. But, that doesn't mean that all the Soul Ages can't benefit from the knowledge of these Elders; they can.

You may be a Mature or Old Soul currently, and you have already declared your intention to be a Seeker in the Seeker School. Or you could be a Transcendental Soul in the Seeker School who decided to return to Earth and refine some of your knowledge. At this time, because the environment on the Earth is under attack in so many ways (oil spills, nuclear waste, whales and dolphins slaughtered by Navy sonar, the list is endless) many Seeker souls are incarnate on the Earth either as "walk-ins" or "birth-ins" to teach humanity to live in greater balance and harmony with each other, and their environment. Also, the Earth is currently giving Seekers the opportunity to witness what not to do; or what will create imbalance. Wherever you are in the Seeker School you can be sure that Merlin is one of your guides.

Just as humans go through Soul Ages, so too does the Earth. She is currently moving from Young Soul to Mature Soul, and this profound shift is being experienced by the life forms that reside upon her. She has consciousness and is not just a rock set out in space, as many have believed. Earth is a created life form and like all other created life forms, she evolves. The damage that has been done on her back with greed and pillaging has caused her to feel used. How like an out-of-balance Young Soul she feels! Many think that as the Earth moves into maturity she may ask for a divorce from those who have wronged her.

## LESSONS FOR YOUNG, MATURE AND OLD SOULS

### YOUNG SOUL LESSONS

**Lesson One for a Young Soul**: Young souls are developing their abilities and honing their skills much like teenagers and young adults do. Therefore, it is important for Young Souls to learn patience and honor the journey and not just the destination. If a Young Soul can put their ego and fears aside, and allow older souls to mentor them, they are very likely to make great strides toward developing their soul's purpose and gifts. It is not uncommon for a Young Soul to be mentored by an older soul; for example, a famous writer, or musician, might mentor a younger person who shares their interest. In this case what most people see is an older man or woman taking the time to teach a younger person; but what they don't realize is that this can also be an older soul lending his or her wisdom to a younger soul.

If you are a Young Soul allow yourself to be mentored, and admit that someone might know more than you and have something to teach you. If you seek out tutelage, and listen to your elders with respect, you will advance quickly. This is the time in the soul's progression to refine the skills and gifts that God gave you, so take advantage of what's available and focus on refining those skills with proper guidance.

**Lesson Two for a Young Soul**: Patience. Because Young Souls traditionally have a great deal of energy they act without reflection. The ego is so strong in a Young Soul that they think they have to do everything all the time, and they don't understand the "let go and let God" principle. They achieve a great deal when they put their mind to it; but sometimes they run over other people they perceive to be in their way. Learning to achieve harmony by allowing things to unfold, and other people to have their way, is an important lesson for a Young Soul to integrate.

Karma creation occurs when you take free will from others and step all over them and learning this definition early on can mitigate some of the karma so prevalent in the Young Soul age. A Young Soul would do well to remember the adage: "What you sow, you reap." Those people you step on while trying to get ahead will come back to haunt you lifetimes later.

**Lesson Three for a Young Soul:** Stop judging others so much; especially by their outward appearance. Young souls tend to see the outside of a person before they look inside, and appearance is traditionally very important to them. Whether they admit it openly or not, most Young Souls are continually sizing up others and deciding whether or not they are worth their time. That trait does not seem to vary much between a Young Soul with a lot of money and prestige, or a Young Soul who has far less and lives in modest surroundings. It might seem logical that a wealthy landowner who lives in a penthouse would be far more likely to judge others based on outside appearances, but this isn't so. For example, a Young Soul who lives in a small trailer park will be just as likely to talk badly about their neighbor because they leave their trash out on the sidewalk, than a wealthy New Yorker who can't abide their friend's new dress and hairstyle.

What is interesting is that this trait can go in exactly the opposite direction in a Young Soul, and they can act almost too sweet all the time. If you have met someone who smiles the brightest smile, and never shows a shadow side, you can be pretty sure that's a Young Soul before you. Think about it; it's the flip side of the coin. Those people are often exhibiting proper social behavior that was taught to them, and they have never questioned. If they were told that they will be more accepted and loved if they act the part of good girl or boy, a Young Soul will work desperately hard to keep up that demeanor all the time. They might become so removed from their real feelings that they never develop an authentic sense of self.

If you are a Young Soul, and you wish not to be judged, and to live in a more harmonious world, you might do well to think before you speak ill about your neighbor for their tacky lawn decorations, and bad taste in automobiles or men. Strive to find what is common between you, instead of what separates you. Most people have many things in common that will bring them closer; break the bad habit of seeing what you don't like, or what separates you, and start to imagine how you are alike instead. If, on the other hand, you are one of those too-sweet types, try speaking your truth now and then. It might make the world a far better place, and liberate others to speak their truth as well.

## MATURE SOUL LESSONS

**Lesson One for a Mature Soul**: A Mature Soul has begun the journey inward, and as they move through this soul age they grasp the concept of mirroring, which means they understand that if something bothers them in someone else, often it is reflecting something they don't like in themselves. Self-help books, seminars, workshops, and soul-searching retreat centers are paid for by Mature Souls who long to find harmony, heal their karma, find their soul mate, and make a living by developing their soul's purpose. Mature Souls often waffle between "I don't know anything," and "I am so enlightened," which puts them on an emotional roller coaster.

Early Mature Souls will still cling to the Young Soul ways, and often be more judgmental. They see the injustice that exists in the world, and their reaction can be to hate everyone who is causing it. They might go to extreme levels of activism and rage before they understand that they hate what's outside of them because they hate what's inside them. That realization often leads them to think that if they fix themselves they will fix the world. In the end they often feel very disappointed when the world isn't getting better, even though they've worked so very hard on themselves.

If a Mature Soul wishes to advance more rapidly in their studies they must stop the workshop merry-go-round and spend time integrating, and processing what all the workshop teachers are teaching. Instead of running off to another workshop to heal yourself, and the world, take the time to listen to what's in your own heart, then integrate the wisdom you've acquired. Your teacher may know what works for them; but may not know the ideal path for you. Learning to listen to yourself, and trust your own intuition, is the job of the Mature Soul.

**Lesson Two for the Mature Soul:** Learn to balance dark and light. Mature souls tend to fall into one of two categories: It's all love and peace, and the bad stuff is an illusion; or it's all crap and screwed up, and nobody can fix this mess. Sometimes they jump on the teeter-totter back and forth between the two.

Because the Mature Soul is processing so much of their earlier soul age karma they can go to extremes as they bring the memories of their past lives to the surface. For example, if a Mature Soul works in an office with someone who they find particularly horrible to deal with, they will search for psychological reasons behind the emotion. They will try to change the dynamic with advice they have read, and oftentimes they will blame themselves for what they are feeling. Whereas a Young Soul would be far more likely to blame the other person for being a bitch, and launch an all-out attack, a Mature Soul will think: *what's wrong with me that I can't get along with her?* Then she will try to change her behavior in a myriad of ways and ponder why it isn't working.

Finally, if they are a late-level Mature Soul, they will begin to see or understand the karma that is causing the emotion, and search out healing techniques to mitigate the karma such as cutting the energy cords between them, or sending them love and forgiveness to change the vibes in the office.

To advance, a Mature Soul must move from self-recrimination and the feeling that the entire world is resting on their shoulders. They must truly integrate the accumulated knowledge, and remember that they have some of the answers within them as they learn to rely on their own instincts. They have to stop making things all good or bad, and realize that in a dualistic reality, such as exists on the Earth, both are going to be living side-by-side. And finally, they have to realize that even if they fix themselves, the guy next to them may be a Baby Soul, and seeing the world through a completely different pair of glasses.

**Lesson Three for the Mature Soul:** Mature Souls must eventually learn that they must love themselves first and foremost. There isn't only one soul mate for you. There isn't only one soul purpose. There isn't only one religion that makes sense. There isn't only one guru you should follow who has the answers. It's okay to say No to other people when you are over-extended.

Mature Souls learn their lessons hard. They find their soul mate only to lose them. They discover their soul purpose, only to find you can't make a living at it. They find the guru you just know is going to lead you to enlightenment, and he has sex with underage minors or your best friend. You think you've got it all together and you fall apart. You're sure that there is a greater purpose, and then it all seems meaningless. You give yourself away to everybody, and then they don't appreciate you.

Yes, you gave, and gave, and gave, and gave, and now you are depleted, and you have to run to another workshop or retreat center, and you feel guilty saying *No* to somebody who just asked yet another favor. Or you have to say *No* to a friend or family member who is an addict, and you feel that you are a bad person for doing it. Or you can't say *No*, and you end up drained dry of energy and you still can't disappoint them. Mature Souls struggle with the notion that they can burn off bad karma, and also love themselves. Non-profit agencies and social work offices are filled with Mature Souls who are burnt out and feel enslaved to the system. They want to help, but the system doesn't appreciate them. Mature Souls have to learn that it's okay to stir things up and demand justice for themselves, not just for everyone else. Find your own voice and then use it to defend *you* once in awhile, that would help the Mature Soul to grow more quickly, and be in less pain as they do it.

## OLD SOUL LESSONS

**Lesson One for the Old Soul:** Stop talking about how much you want to leave the Earth plane. This is a trait shared by Mature Souls as well; especially late-level Mature Souls. Stop thinking that you've been through the mill and you can't imagine why you are still here; this is a trait shared by arrogant Young Souls who think they are more advanced than they are. Stop thinking that if you have to listen to one more idiotic person you are going to shoot yourself, or them. That's a trait shared by every soul age now and then except the too-sweet Young Souls.

The Old Souls are ready to depart. They've tried to fix everything in the Mature Soul age, they've healed most of their darkest karma, and they are just cleaning up the last pieces of the karma they missed before they get to exit for good. (An Old Soul will sometimes say, "Thank God, I am almost out of here," which is often a hard sentiment for a Young or Baby Soul to grasp.)

Sorry, Old Soul, there is still self-karma. Damn, you mean I've got to learn to love myself? Sigh . . . really? Sigh . . . Come on! Haven't I done enough already? Haven't I paid my dues? I've loved, I've hated, I've warred, I've waged peace . . . please give me a break and just let me off this crazy Earth! Please! Love myself? I love myself. Really, I promise. I love the fact that I'm forty pounds overweight. Except when I look at myself in a bathing suit, and all those Young Souls are judging me; then I judge myself too. I even loved myself when I didn't get that job because I was too old . . . except I saw the way that thirty-year-old, snot-faced kid looked at me like he knew everything, and how he thought I was too old to be "with it."

Oh, No! They will now be in self-judgment because they didn't, "Love thy neighbor as thyself!" (Or maybe they did, because neither one was getting much love.) What a lot of pressure the Old Soul often feels, before they learn to relax a little.

Everyone has this notion that Old Souls are these noble beings who walk around with deep furrows in their brows because they are so wise; or they have eyes that are pools of infinite love and wisdom, or they never say a bad word about themselves or anyone else. In short everyone has a fantasy that an Old Soul is perfect, and just waiting to float off the Earth plane without struggle because they know something other people don't. Wrong!

Old Souls are human like everyone else. They *have* been through the mill, that's true. But, how many people really like to listen to old people? Old people are placated in this Young-Soul society, but not really revered. Old souls are often treated the same way, because Old Souls are finally learning to speak their truth. They won't always say what you want to hear, but they will say what you need to hear, or at the very least, they will say what they think you need to hear. Old Souls, like old people, finally learn that it doesn't matter half as much if the guy next to you likes you, what matters is that you like yourself. Old Souls have seen how the lies in our society create more hell realm for everyone than the truth. Old Souls know that the hardest thing to do is to look in the mirror and say, "I love you."

An Old Soul knows that no one really wants to hear what they have to say, because they won't give easy answers, or a panacea to what ails you. Old Souls are never feel-good doctors on TV, and they don't tell you to always look on the bright side because it makes you feel better; or tell you that your pain is just an illusion that you are better off ignoring. They will acknowledge the truth of your suffering simultaneously with the truth that not suffering also exists as a possibility. Old Souls don't judge others as crazy because they have had an experience that belies what society believes is possible. Tell an Old Soul that you just had tea with the President, or flew in a spaceship, and they will say, "Really? Tell me about it." Old Souls are truly the kings and queens of "whatever," but not because they behave like sassy teenagers who think you are too stupid to be bothered with. Old Souls say "whatever" because they know that anything is possible, and why argue with someone else's definition of reality?

They also do not become politicians; but occasionally they become leaders. Old Souls will lead or become famous when they can do so by stating their truth without compromise; for that is what they must learn. They must learn to love themselves enough to stand by their truth, even in the face of public denial.

Old Souls must eliminate the last shreds of fear, because they realize that fear stands in the way of them loving themselves, and others, and moving forward. For that reason Old Souls will never deny the existence of darkness. Old Souls will wrestle with the devil, stare him down, and realize that they must learn to be free of all fear, and that includes him. Old Souls don't deny the devil, as others do; they have seen him face-to-face, and even then they don't back down. Old Souls teach that love, not human love, but a love much greater than that, releases you from fear. Old Souls begin to grasp the *We Are All One* reality in a way that other soul ages can't. Like an old man, or woman, sits in a nursing home and realizes that all the foolish striving of their younger years ended up with this, an Old Soul lets go of their human identity, and begins to embrace a new, larger sense of self.

I suppose in the end there is no point telling an Old Soul what to work on, because they already know what they have to do. If you tried to tell an Old Soul what they should be doing to better themselves they might nod their head politely, but you can be sure they will not have listened to a word you said. An Old Soul has at last learned to follow their heart. When an Old Soul has completed their last Earthly incarnation they advance to what is known as Transcendental Soul, and they are now learning without physically incarnating onto the Earth, unless they choose to. When a Transcendental Soul incarnates on Earth, it is often to accomplish a mission. The Buddhists have a word for this: Bodhisattva. This is a soul who has taken a vow to reincarnate until all souls are free of the karmic wheel. This is a Transcendental Soul who continually reincarnates to teach, or mirror, a higher truth.

From the point of view of a Transcendental Soul, time is not linear. An easier way to understand this is to imagine that your Transcendental Soul (or Higher Self) sits at the hub of a very large wheel, and many spokes emanate from the hub. The spokes represent your many incarnations. When you are sitting in the middle of the wheel all the spokes (or incarnations) can be seen at once. When you are on the rim of the wheel, you can only see one spoke (or life) at a time.

Full membership into the Seeker School is achieved at the Transcendental Soul age but, as previously mentioned, Earth is a teaching ground for these souls, and although not every Earth human will become a Seeker, every Seeker will have done a full reincarnation cycle on the Earth. The biodiversity that is found on Earth is quite unique, and it affords Seekers the opportunity to spend enormous amounts of time interacting with other biological life forms. It also allows them the opportunity to experience life in the body of these life forms, and so a Seeker's incarnations are not exclusive to human ones. If you are Seeker soul you can be pretty sure that you have had a wide variety of experiences. As part of your training you have had the opportunity to experience life as everything from ant, to beetle, to dolphin, and even rocks and trees. In other words, your consciousness has been connected to all of these life forms, and more, at one time or another.

Seekers and Starseeds are often drawn to working with environmental issues, and in professions that involve animal welfare, and they feel tremendous pain at the abuse suffered on this planet. They understand intuitively that the human race is not to be thought of as superior, and that ownership of land and animals is a consciousness that leads to destruction and war. How many wars have been fought over land? How many animals have become extinct due to humans hunting them into oblivion? A Seeker will be repulsed by these actions because they are involved in a school that studies balance of elements, not domination.

Seekers (and Starseeds) must be willing to step-up to the plate and take leadership positions, but, due to the corruption of the institutions on the Earth, many of them run from those responsibilities, and would rather hide in the shadows than be seen. Another reason many do not wish to be noticed is because they have suffered abuse in previous lives, and fear that they will suffer again. Because Earth is such a harsh schoolroom, those who want to help often cannot release their fear enough to do their job. Unfortunately, that means that the ones who take the reins of government, and other institutions of control, are often those whose hearts are not so soft and who do not have compassion for those outside of their circle of concern.

The "dog-eat-dog world," created by the Reptilian, lower mind, frightens the Seeker (and many Starseeds) into submission. There have been those who have been able to speak out against injustice, even in the face of their own demise. But, far too often in the past, when they stood up for what they felt was right, they were tortured, burned, and imprisoned, and so they are naturally afraid of doing this again. Learning to speak your truth, and understanding that you can never be fully in your power until you do, is a difficult but necessary lesson for modern-day Seekers and Starseeds. They must learn the lesson: In every experience there is a gift and a blessing so that they do not fall into victim consciousness.

**EXERCISE TWO:** Close your eyes and sit in a quiet and undisturbed place. No music, or noise, unless the noise is the sound of nature. After about ten or fifteen minutes of quiet ask yourself this question: What is my soul age? What do I need to work on right now? Am I a Seeker soul? Am I a Starseed? Then ask Merlin to give you a "knowing." Be patient. He will.

# Chapter Three

## *Know Thyself: Integration Of The Soul*

The most important event that marks a first-year student's entrance into the Seeker school is the assignment of a primary teacher. A primary teacher is a Seeker school graduate who has decided to specialize in assisting other Seekers and their studies. The adage on Earth, "Those who can't do, teach," is not the point of view of those who work in Merlin's school. Here teachers are revered and honored, and with the guidance of their primary teacher each Seeker will be required to revisit their many incarnations (on Earth and elsewhere) prior to beginning their studies.

(Please understand that the term "first-year student" is tongue-in-cheek as time is not measured in years once one moves from linear Earth time.)

Step one is becoming fully awake. The maze of lives on Earth, and elsewhere, has often left the soul feeling incomplete, and it is imperative that a soul be re-integrated before they even think about stepping foot into the Seeker's classroom. It is fully understood that the Seeker must be required to *Know Thyself,* and these words are written not only above the Temple of Delphi, but also above the entrance to the Seeker's school. Whereas on Earth humans are continually telling one another what to do, think, or be, without spending even a moment on self-reflection, in the Seeker school self-reflection is considered to be a soul's most important task.

A human body contains merely a fragment of the full expression of its Transcendental Soul. It is important to understand that the Transcendental Soul is the reintegrated soul. The Transcendental Soul houses all the pieces and parts that have explored lives throughout time and space. A Transcendental Soul has collected experiences and information through its fragments, evolved those fragments to the fullest possible, and then re-formed itself in its entirety. The wisdom that all pieces of the self have gathered must be integrated and digested before the soul begins its studies as a Seeker. A Transcendental Soul is therefore a bigger soul than the soul fragment that occupies most human bodies. Within an individual human is merely the fragment of the larger soul, and rarely does a fully-reintegrated Transcendental Soul choose to reincarnate upon the Earth. Occasionally, however, it does, but it will never reincarnate upon the Earth without a mission and purpose to be fulfilled.

If any piece of the soul has not been fully integrated, or healed, because of a traumatic event, special attention will be paid by the Seeker's teacher to do what is necessary to reconcile that experience. What might be interesting to many of you is that a Seeker might specialize in the areas which have proven most problematic during their incarnations. For example, a soul will often repeat, over and over, a story or path, almost obsessively, throughout many incarnations. Those of you who have begun the work of past life reflection have found this to be exactly true. Not only have you come to understand that you have become trapped over and over in the same story on Earth; but those of you evolved enough to have explored your extra-planetary lives, have found that the karma you created throughout the galaxies followed you onto the Earth, and was repeated and revisited during your many lives.

Rather than seeing this as entrapment, it can be helpful to say that each fragment specializes in a particular area, and so repeats and repeats lessons around that concept. One soul fragment may specialize in greed, while another will specialize in self-destruction. Each of these soul fragments can then bring all they have learned about their specialty back to the table to teach the re-integrated soul all it knows. A soul fragment will often learn by alternating between both the positive and negative poles, however, some soul fragments may enjoy learning primarily through the positive pole, while others may enjoy the negative pole. If the fragment is learning about greed they may choose in one life to learn by being generous, and then in another life they will experience its polar opposite, greed.

A Seeker who has experienced a great deal of poverty and starvation might become interested in being a life creator of herbs, fruits or vegetables, and wish to study the balance of nature with respect to feeding and life sustenance. Or they might be interested in creating a species that will not be dependent on constant feeding as they were on Earth; one that might be able to go long periods without food or water. You can imagine that certain Earth species were indeed created with just that in mind.

Without the reintegration of the soul it is impossible to move forward as a more enlightened being. A soul in the state of fragmentation is a soul disempowered. This is not to say that the dissemination of the soul fragments throughout time and space, to gather experiences, is not only necessary but advantageous, because it is, but until a soul reintegrates itself, much of the knowledge will remain outside of the fragment's grasp. In other words, the vast majority of humans will never have access to all the knowledge contained within all their soul fragments.

However, because the question, "Who am I?" is a question asked by so many humans, it could be quite advantageous to the development of each human to gather as many pieces of their soul as their consciousness can hold while still on Earth. Most humans believe that it is not possible to remember past lives, but in actuality the opposite is true. The human mind is continually fighting with itself not to remember, and the natural urge is to awaken and remember at least a portion of the soul's experiences. The amount of energy required to forget who one is taxes the human organism a great deal. If human beings were allowed access to even a tiny portion of their wisdom the soul would relax, because the search to *Know Thyself* would not be so all pervasive.

The amount of diversion created on Earth, through mindless games and pastimes, is done primarily to keep humans from the fear they feel because they don't know who they are, or why they exist. The gaping hole of fear that threatens to swallow up most humans is overwhelming as they stare into space and feel so alone. Earthlings await the arrival of "men from space," completely unaware that they are what they have been awaiting.

God cannot know itself until it has something to mirror back to itself. Thus the soul was created. The creation of the soul occurred when a piece of consciousness knew itself to be other. When God is One Thing, He/She cannot contemplate itself. When God creates something that appears to be other, then God knows itself. When one returns to the Source, and disappears within It, the soul disappears. To explain that more easily, if you are the reflection in the mirror of God, when the reflection in the mirror jumps into God, then the reflection ceases to exist.

So, one of the first things a Seeker understands is that all things are a reflection of him/herself. A Seeker understands that all people in the Seeker's world are a mirror reflection of the Self; just as the Seeker is a reflection of God. In the search to *Know Thyself*, the Seeker understands that they must use the mirror God has given them to understand who they are. Human Seekers will begin to grasp this idea, and use it to understand their own motivations more clearly. For example, your Mother and Father are often mirror reflections of your own strengths and weaknesses, and a true Seeker is always aware that they chose their parents to reflect something back to them that they needed to see. A Young Soul will blame their parents for being something; an older soul will ask, "What did my parent reflect back to me?" Are you overly critical? Are you aggressive? Are you too passive? Are you fearful? Do you hate that in others? Then you hate it in yourself. You cannot hate "it" in others if you do not hate "it" in yourself as well. Conversely, you cannot love in others what you do not love in yourself. You are a mirror for them; they are a mirror for you. This is truly the meaning of One World, and the idea of "as above, so below, and "as inside, so outside."

Perhaps you are now saying, "I hate murderers, and I am not a murderer." But, you are a murderer. You have been a murderer in other lives. If you have gone to war you have been a murderer, and you can be sure that you have had at least one life where you went to war, since human history is the history of warfare. The need humans have to kill one another bothers you deeply. Then you can be sure you have experienced it, if not in this life, in others. You have seen how fear and rage leads to murder, and you are repulsed by your past experiences. You hate that in yourself, and you hate it in others. You hate those who remind you of what you already know but want to forget. There is nothing on this Earth that isn't a reflection of what you know. There is nothing that isn't a reflection of what God knows. God knows what you know.

There are those who want to separate you from God by telling you that you know things that God doesn't know. If this is true, then who are you? If you are not an extension of God, then who do you belong to? Those who wish to keep you weak, and separate from the One God, will lie to you, and tell you that God does not know you; those who wish you to be strengthened in the arms of God will tell you that God knows you intimately because you are God—a piece and a part of the Living God.

A Seeker must integrate and understand their soul fragments, and love and accept all parts of the self. This is the job of the primary teacher. When acceptance of all parts of the self is complete, and all fragments have been returned and loved, then the Seeker is ready to go to school.

The amount of time required to prepare the soul for school will differ from student-to-student, and there are no limits placed on the teacher, or student, in the completion of the task.

**EXERCISE THREE:** When we step from victim consciousness, into mastery, we recognize that we choose our parents prior to incarnating. This realization demands that we look deeper into that relationship; we must ask ourselves why.

Here is an exercise to deepen self-awareness: Ask yourself what your mother and father mirror for you. What do you dislike in them? What do you admire in them? How does this reflect back to you? Do the same for your husband or wife. Do the same for your children. Despite what many people believe, prior to incarnating they chose you, and you chose them. What do you reflect back for them? What do you have to learn from one another? For many people one parent will often mirror their shadow, while the other their light. If this resonates for you, then ask yourself how you might evolve past this duality, and find greater neutrality and harmony within yourself.

If you are a Mature Soul, you are involved in some heavy karmic clean-up, but you have the tools to approach the task with awareness, rather than victim mentality. Begin the journey of karmic awareness with past life regression, and forgiveness of karmic debt. If you are an Old Soul you are involved not only in clearing some past life karmic debris, but in integrating and loving all parts of yourself. This time in human history offers the opportunity for enormous personal growth if you are willing to take up the challenge.

What pieces of yourself have you rejected that you need to love and accept? Can you look in a mirror and love what you see, not just physically, but in all ways? Do you reject others because they reveal your own shadow? These are some difficult questions to answer.

In summary we might say that Exercise Three is: *Know thyself* and *Love thyself.*

# Chapter Four

## *Collaborating With The Angelic Realm*

The great archangels are available to everyone. That means you! Unlike what many people have been raised to believe, the archangels, along with guardian angels, love to assist humans as they journey through life. Recognizing when they are with you, and learning their individual energetic imprint, is your responsibility. Angels are not there to tell you what to believe, what to do, or to predict the future. They will not live your life for you; but they will keep you working from your Higher Self, if you utilize them to be companions. The archangels do not tell humanity what to do; instead they illuminate the truth so that human beings can decide what they will *choose* to do about a situation.

If an entity declares itself to be angelic, and yet bosses you around, or makes you feel less than, it is not a true angelic energy. Entities can mask themselves and pretend to be angelic; but angels are not voices in your head, instead they embody energy that liberates and illuminates. Do not confuse these great angelic energies with your human relatives who have passed. Angels and human ghosts are vastly different, and when accessed they will respond in their own unique ways.

When working with angelic energy you are working with your Higher Mind. Accessing these beings assists you into greater neutrality, unconditional love, and past fear responses that crop up in relationship to life's challenges. They offer another tool to gaining a higher point of view on an issue. They are not an escapist elixir to be used to avoid your issues, but as guides to help you face your fears and overcome them. They can provide relief from tension, stress and strain and remind you how to bring love to a difficult situation.

A human soul who has passed will offer a more limited human perspective. If your grandmother always wanted you to go to church it could be likely that when she passes, and contacts you, her message will remain the same: "Go to church." That is unless she has decided upon passing that church is actually unnecessary and God is everywhere and in everything, due to a revelation received on the other side. But, in most cases, Grandma's message will often be quite similar to what she would deliver when she was incarnated upon the Earth. In other words, a relative can still have the same point of view even after they have passed from the human body. An archangel will never tell you what to do. It is the job of the angels to illuminate truth for humanity; what we do with the truth is up to us. Even when you want an angel to be bossy, they will never say something such as, "Go to church." Instead they will challenge you to recognize your truth, speak your truth, and be in integrity with love and compassion.

True archangels are strong energies: Forgiveness, Wisdom, Knowledge, Protection, Communication, Relationship, Self-Adoration, Peace, Serenity and so forth. They hold the apex of these energies, and ask you to consider your life from the highest aspect of these ideals. They are not easy to be with because they know who you are; but fortunately for us, they understand our foibles, and they love us despite our very human issues. However, they do not support victim consciousness, or lying and dishonesty. They are quite clear that such behavior will not lead a human being anywhere but into a lot of trouble. Still, they won't tell you what to do and they must respect your free will and your right to learn the hard way.

Developing a personal and clear relationship with the Angelic realm is essential for a Seeker of wisdom and truth. Learning who to call on, and how to access them, will bring your human ego-based consciousness closer to your Higher Consciousness. You cannot hear angels, or feel angels, or know angels, without quiet respect and meditation time. It is not that they abandon you during times of difficulty and stress; but the energy they carry is so subtle that it is difficult to feel their presence unless you are making room for them to quietly, and gently, touch your heart. True angels do not barge in on your life, instead they gently hold your highest ideals in readiness for you to embody and remember.

Making a heart-link is the first and most important thing you can do to make contact with the archangels. In order to achieve proper alignment it is important that the seven on-body chakras be balanced. The chakras are the energy centers located from the base of the spine to the crown of the head, and they glow with the colors of the rainbow. Balance your chakras (red, orange, yellow, green, and blue, indigo, violet) and then sit quietly with your heart chakra wide open. Imagine a golden ball of light in your heart and send that light up above your head, and into your angel's heart. Allow your angel to send heart energy back to your heart, and link. Feel the flow of energy move through your body and out into the world.

As a Seeker you are a student of subtle energy and you have learned, or are learning, to perceive the unseen realms with clarity and assurance. Working with the angelic realm is an aspect of this energy, and all healers will be working (either consciously or unconsciously) with angelic energy. Few doctors or nurses in hospital settings will acknowledge the presence of angels but rest assured they are in every nook and cranny of every hospital, whether the doctor is aware of them or not. Because angels must respect free will, they will not interfere unless asked to do so, or unless the patient, or family and friends, request intervention.

Energy healers who are working within the highest principles are automatically connected to the angelic realm, although they may or may not be aware of the energies assisting them. It is your job to familiarize yourself with these energies, and close the gap between heaven and Earth. The major archangels are a good place to begin. Here are some of the most common that can aid you in your work as a healer, Seeker, and along the path of life.

1. **Archangel Michael**: Known as the Angel of Protection, Archangel Michael is a powerful energy of light, and carries the energy of the warrior. His ability to cut through negative energy is symbolized by the

sword he carries. When called upon he will bring a Legion of Angels to clean and clear negative, demonic, or dark force energies, and surround you with Light. Ask him to ring your body with his blue flame of protection, and visualize that nothing can get past this barrier. When Archangel Michael is around you may see intense blue flashes of light, which lets you know he is surrounding you with protection and love.

2. **Archangel Raphael**: Known as the Angel of Healing, he will bring healing energy to any situation that requires it. His Legions work in hospitals, clinics and healing centers to assist humans to find balance and harmony within themselves, and their environment. Raphael will help you to understand what lies beneath the illness. He knows that for illness to manifest in the physical body it must first manifest in the subtle, energetic body. Because of this he will reveal to you the root cause of the illness; whether it lies in a past life or in the current one. Raphael glows with a green color, signifying the energy of love and vibrating with the heart chakra.

3. **Archangel Gabriel**: Known as the Angel of Communication, it is Gabriel who often assists us with our soul purpose, manifesting needs that support that purpose, and understanding why we are being guided to do one thing or another. He will present a torch to you when you have taken up your soul's purpose, signifying his support that lights your way. Working consciously with the Archangel Gabriel will assist you to understand clearly the root cause of any troubling issue, and why you feel stuck.

4. **Archangel Metatron**: Known as the Keeper of the Akashic Records, or Library of God, he guards the great halls and will lead you on a journey to discovering who you are. In meditation if you ask him to give you entry to the Hall of Records he will meet you at the door and invite you inside. Upon entrance he will lead you to the *Book of Your Lives*, and allow you to open the book to reveal a past life. Also, if you are comfortable with sacred geometry, and enjoy communicating with symbols and abstract images, Metatron may work well with your path. Use him in your journey of self-discovery.

5. **Archangel Ariel**: The Angel of Mother Nature, she works with the Earth-based energies such as fairies and elves. If you resonate with the animal and nature realms you are already working with Archangel Ariel. Animal lovers and nature lovers, as well as those working to assist Mother Earth with environmental issues, are automatically working with Ariel and her teams.

6. **Archangel Chamuel**: Chamuel's energy is like rich, honey-gold syrup light which coats your mind, body and spirit with gentle and loving frequencies. Her job is to remind you how cherished you are by God, and teach you to cherish and respect yourself. When you are feeling down and depressed call on Chamuel for assistance to bring you back to your loving and positive nature. Unlike some of the more powerful angelic energies, Chamuel will never overpower you, but instead give you the grace you seek.

7. **Archangel Uriel**: Uriel is a strong presence and will bring karmic issues into focus, assisting you to find peace with tragedy, and help to calm difficult relationships. Uriel will minister to you when trouble seems all around you, giving you the faith and wisdom you need to rectify the situation. Call on Uriel when all hope seems lost, and he will give you the strength you need to carry on.

So, here are a few of the major archangels. Many of you are already working with some, if not all of them. Allow others to join your team as well, and learn to feel their frequencies in and around your body. Instead of reaching outward to the angels, begin to allow their energy into your body so that you feel their presence within your heart. When you feel a tingle on your scalp, or on your skin, you can be sure the angels are letting you know that your (or another's) words are truth.

These archangels are powerful beings, and it is important that you do not relegate them to the position of being wimpy little wisps. Far from it, these energies are bringers of truth, and will awaken your consciousness in profound and challenging ways. They stand guard at the doorway of your highest vision of the world. This does not mean that they live in "la-la" land; they are well aware of human suffering and injustice. But, in order to serve us, it is their job to keep open the door to heaven, so that we may find it whether still alive on Earth, or in the afterlife.

While the majority of humans pray to them, and reach out to angels as distant, remote, and often inaccessible beings, Seekers will draw close to the angelic realm and make true friends of these heavenly companions. Experiment with their energies, and dialogue with them. But, do not mistake a voice in your head for an angelic nudge. Angels to not tell you what to do or think; instead they open the crown chakra, the third eye, and the heart, so that you will have the inner knowing of what is the right use of will. In that way they serve as our conscience, holding us to proper behavior.

There are humans who hold the energies of the angelic beings: these humans are the emanations of the great archangels. It might help to understand that they are a tiny piece of the archangel, sent to earth to hold the frequency of the angel. Some examples are, the Angel of Beauty (Iofiel), the Angel of Blessings (Amarushaya), the angel of Grace (Ananchel). These humans are meant to embody, on Earth, the emanations of these great archangels, to assist humanity to remember their Higher Selves.

The heavenly spheres are actually quite sophisticated, and it is important to realize that not all angels are exactly like other angels. Humans have categorized angels into various groupings: First Sphere: Seraphim, Cherubim and Thrones. Second Sphere: Dominions, Virtues and Powers. Third Sphere: Principalities, Archangels, Angels. But, angels are not class conscious and do not place greater or lesser value upon one another. They view one another as fulfilling a purpose and a need; each being essential to the task at hand. Archangels and Angels, belonging to the Third Sphere, are closer to the Earth, and so humans have easier access to them. In other words, they serve human interests quite well. If you have not done so already, begin from this moment on to see angels as your friends, and companions, and include them in your life every day.

**EXERCISE FOUR**: If you already work with the archangels listed earlier then expand your angelic repertoire. Connect to Cassiel, Hamied, Raziel, Remliel, and Sandalphon without any preconceived notion of what they do, or how they feel. Discover for yourself who these angels are by asking each one: What is your duty? What energy to you embody? How can I best work with you? How will I know you are around me? In your journal record the answers and expand the information as you work with the angels every day. They are there to help you, so ask them for their wisdom and insight.

# Chapter Five

## *Creation On And Off Earth*

You are first and foremost a creational being. It is impossible to be alive and not create. Even an act of destruction is an act of creation. In general (with some exceptions) the youngest soul ages create with less mental stress around the act of creation. That compares to young children. To a child, creating something seems as natural as breathing in and out; and tribal cultures integrate art into their lives in ways that more sophisticated societies often do not. Becoming self-conscious about your creations blocks the pure energy of creation and most artists will explain that they must get their self-judging ego out of the way in order for the energy of creation to flow freely through them.

Over time, as human beings became more sophisticated, and developed cultural identities, their creations reflected that. Rather than depict what they were looking at through literal reproduction, they began to use symbols to take the place of an actual object, or they represented the personality or emotional state of something by distorting its shape or face to reflect a deeper wisdom. As human beings have evolved, so too have their artistic and technological creations. The greatest artists have learned that they must balance technique and inspiration to bring something to life. It is not enough to play the correct keys on a piano; one must also infuse the music with much more to make the performance exciting. A good artist has mastered technique so they can get their ego-mind out of the way enough to let pure creative energy flow through them.

Artists love to create because it brings them closer to the God-Source. An atheist will not use those words, of course, but they experience the same high. Being infused with pure creational energy is an ecstatic experience. Those who choose the Seeker's path understand this ecstasy, and are drawn to become life creators because they love being in a state of conscious creation with the Energy that Infuses All. Seekers understand that the mastering of technique is essential to becoming a Master Life Creator, much as any artist understands that they must study technique before they earn the freedom to inspire or entertain. Nobody wants to listen to a singer hit all the wrong notes, or watch a ballerina fall off her toe shoes.

While artists are quicker to notice how this creational force called God races through them, and will even acknowledge their attraction to the energy, scientists, inventors, and many other professions receive a similar high while in the act of creation, but are less likely to speak about it. In the spiritual realm Merlin has outlined the requirements a soul must meet before they are given the responsibility for life creation, but on Earth there is really no regulation at all. As a result the energy can easily become corrupted, and a scientist can torture animals and humans to test their hypothesis; or create merely to achieve an end that is powered by greed. Humans have done a poor job of self-regulation in these matters, and have paid a high price for their out-of-balance creational urges. From a spiritual point of view, it indicates a complete disrespect for the God-Source, and humans have come up with many justifications to explain their motivations.

Now that you understand a bit more about how various Soul Ages operate, it is easy to imagine that a Young or Baby-Soul scientist would be far less likely to be concerned about how their creation is impacting the greater good. Native American Elders taught that it was essential for every generation to think of the impact their creations would have on the seventh generation in the future. Currently, CEOs and world leaders can barely fathom more than a few months into the future. Teaching children to think about their children's children is wise, but rarely done.

If humans understood that they are given the sacred duty to be God-like creators, they would be far less likely to misuse the power of creation. It is the job of the Mature and Old Soul Seekers to teach the younger soul ages how to create in balance; but because most Mature and Older souls have chosen over the last two thousand years to stay out of positions of responsibility and authority, they have allowed the power-hungry younger souls to take over the political arenas, and dictate a reality that has led to their own disempowerment. It has even become popular to look upon world leaders with disdain, and disrespect, because of their gross misuse of power. Until the human race re-establishes a respect for elders of all types (soul age and numerical age) the positions of power will continue to be held by Baby and Young souls and everyone will pay the price.

For some time now, the world of the material, and the world of the spiritual, has been separated by a belief system that teaches the spiritual initiate to draw away from the ordinary world to achieve enlightenment. Monastical life of all traditions encourages the aspirant to give up all ties to the physical world to avoid being sullied by it. This has left the physical world in the hands of those who often have no spiritual interests, or relegate the world of the spiritual to something light, meaningless, and filled with illusions. The spiritual Seekers, and the physical world, must re-join if the old paradigm is to shift. Separation between the physical and the spiritual world has not, in the long run, been of assistance to either side. Unification begins when the spiritual community re-embraces their place on the physical Earth plane, and both government and corporate leaders consider higher principles of consciousness, such as compassion, to have value.

It is important for Seeker students to awaken to their mission, despite the brain-washing that they received from the Dark Energies, whose job it is to deceive. The mission is not just to feel good all the time, but to impact, teach, and guide. First of all, Seekers are equipped with exactly what they need to do their job, even though they are often unaware of the fact. It's the proverbial "clear as the nose on your face." A Seeker and Starseed's gifts have been evident since childhood.

In order for Seekers and Starseeds to get their power, and clarity of vision, back they must release themselves from their fears; this is easier said than done, of course, but fear leads to self-deception. Self-deception leads to two extremes: self-doubt and self-aggrandizement, and neither one of these states of mind supports creation in balance.

Self-doubt can lead to mistakes. Either the person will over compensate and reach beyond their capabilities, or they will be too easily swayed by others, and be susceptible to disruptive influences. Seekers have chosen a sacred, but often challenging path, and there is no place for the misuse of ego in their journey.

If a Seeker or Starseed becomes caught up in what others think of them they will spend too much time comparing themselves to "normal" humans. As a result they might judge themselves as superior (or inferior) and fall sway to dark and deceptive energies. Many Starseeds have known they had gifts since they were little children, but they shut them down when their parents or schoolmates made fun of them, or warned them that they were being possessed. It's not a Starseed's job to worry about what others think of them, and regardless of your soul age, take a tip from your Old Soul brethren and speak your truth despite what others think of you. Those of you who have spoken your truth know how empowered you feel when you do. Those of you who are living lives separate from your truth know how it disempowers you to do so.

Your job is to be an integrated being. As you recall, when a Seeker first enters the Transcendental Seeker School the first thing their Primary Teacher will do is assist them to integrate all the pieces and parts of themselves from their many incarnations. Of course, one human body cannot hold all the pieces and parts of the collective soul, but integration can begin on Earth, and being integrated as a human being means being honest with yourself and others. If you are a different person everywhere you go, and lying to others about who you are, eventually you will disintegrate. Being disintegrated is being disempowered, and you can never manifest and develop your Seeker gifts if you are in such a state.

As a result, it is essential that you are honest with yourself about whether you are living a life of honesty and integration, or a life where you hide your truth to please (or to fool) others. If you are not living in your truth, make a pledge to yourself to begin today. If you are living in your truth, true family, and true friends, will support the vision you have of yourself in the world.

It has become popular to explore the notion that you create your own reality with your thoughts. Certainly you can't expect someone who has the mantra, "The world is a terrible place to be," to create a beautiful and serene environment. It would be impossible. It is important to recognize is that the mantra you carry within you arises from the accumulation of your experiences from many lifetimes, and that you brought it in with you. Your current life is reflecting what you believed prior to incarnating in this lifetime. For some of you this might be a challenging idea, but it is accurate. Because life on Earth has contained tremendous challenges throughout history, and you have struggled with slavery, sexual abuse, starvation, disease, pain and war, it is common for all of you to hold these fears in your unconscious when you reincarnate.

Your death drama from your previous life will be re-established during your birth drama in your current life. You can see the dilemma that a mother might have with the thought she creates her own reality; she might be planning a peaceful water birth and end up with an emergency C-section. The incoming soul's reality is impacting her reality in this case, and the incoming soul appears to win. Reality is mutable but you are not the only one creating it. In Masaru Emoto's water-glass experiments which he documents in his book, *Messages from Water*, he alone is in control of the message being sent to the water molecules; but if three or four people are sending conflicting messages into the water at the same time, the reality created by the molecules reflects all their beliefs.

So, your reality is not only being impacted by the consciousness carried by people throughout the world, but by the unconscious beliefs you are carrying from previous lifetimes. It is delightful that human beings are waking up to their ability to impact their reality, but they must remember that on Earth they are involved in a collective consciousness. This misunderstanding can lead a younger soul to misinterpret the idea of reality creation, and they can adopt an air of superiority when they think they are above the fray. They might blame others for having difficulties, and lose compassion. Subsequently, they blame themselves when something bad happens. This can lead to harsh self-judgment, and to not giving themselves the love and support they so deserve. All human beings learn by trial and error, and one of the fastest ways a child learns is by doing something that harms them. They learn not to do that again! Aren't all humans on the Earth to learn what does and doesn't work? Why then should it be any different for a soul's journey through time and space?

Your reality reflects a complex act of creation, and one that will involve your current beliefs, your family beliefs, your cultural beliefs, and the world's collective consciousness. The molecules are responding to everyone's thought patterns and actions, not just yours.

It is important to understand that reality on the Earth is held in both the third and the fourth dimensional realms. (And certainly, in theory, all dimensions are available to all human beings.) These two dimensions of consciousness are called the Lower Astral realms. The third dimension is the seen realm and the fourth dimension is the unseen realm. Both of these are real and both impact your life. That means that ghosts, demons, spirit guides and even angels, (who exist above the fourth dimension) are impacting everyone's reality, and can have a profound impact on what a person does.

An energetic attachment from the unseen realm will not adhere to, or influence a human being, unless there is a consciousness match. These attachments are not random, and if you are being affected by something from the unseen realms it is because in some manner you have called it to you. This does not mean that your conscious mind wants to have this entity or energy attachment, but it does mean that your unconscious (perhaps even lifetimes ago) made the attachment. If you have an intense drama with someone you can be sure that there is energy attached not only to the event, but that energetic cords have been created that tie you together. Karma is the word given to describe these energy bonds, and karma will draw you together with a person with whom you have unfinished business. The purpose of this connection is so that you will resolve your karma, and awaken to a higher understanding of the event.

For example, if you killed someone in a jealous rage in another life, the karmic triangle will be repeated in a future life. Sometimes, in the case of a Baby or even Young Soul, the energy of revenge would be too prevalent, and the eye-for-an-eye belief system would win out, causing even more karma to be created. Karma can have layers upon layers, and a soul may have an enormous challenge in front of them when they face it again, but the older the soul age, the more likely it will be that the karma will be peacefully forgiven. You may have to re-experience the event again; but this time you must forgive your spouse and her lover, and let them go without enacting revenge. All of this is impacting your reality, and you chose to deal with the karma you face prior to each incarnation.

As a soul matures they become more and more aware of their karma. They may begin to intuitively realize that it is not just one lifetime impacting them. How many times have you felt like you knew that person forever, even though you just met? How many times have you been drawn to, or repulsed by, someone you hardly know? These reactions are the impact of karma, and not to be overlooked or ignored by a Seeker. A Seeker must learn to recognize their own triggers, and ultimately must train the self to tap into their past lives, if they wish to gain a deeper understanding of who they are, and what they are trying to accomplish.

Many times a person will become wedded to victimization because they were a ruthless perpetrator in another life, and they are punishing themselves for their misdeeds. The punishment often becomes a habit, and instead of balancing the karma in a positive and helpful fashion for all the parties involved, the soul plays out the role of victim over and over, relentlessly. Other times a soul will shy away from taking back their power because they have witnessed how power-hungry people have harmed others; which causes a natural aversion to power. There are many people who equate power with bad energy, and will be meek and mild as a result: "The meek shall inherit the Earth" consciousness. Having a voice and standing up for what you feel is right does not make you evil. It is the manner in which you hold power that determines whether you are misusing it or not. If you are stuck in this victimization consciousness you could be drawing bad things to you over and over and wonder why.

What stops you from accessing your past lives is primarily fear. This is the fear that you will discover something about yourself, or another person, that is upsetting to you. But, a true Seeker seeks truth and will not hesitate to hunt it down and meet it face-to-face. Ego has no place in the journey and if you find yourself creating a past life reality that doesn't make sense with your current life, the chances are that you are not being completely honest about the information you are receiving. In order to seek truth the mirror must be your friend, not your enemy.

Sometimes souls will connect to famous people, and believe that they are the reincarnation of these people and it appears that they are making it all up. Past life records are, in truth, available to everyone and certainly anyone can access these famous people. Also, the energy of these individuals is enormous and it could be advantageous for many people to carry their energetic imprints. If the karma a famous soul carries is too much for their individual soul to clean up, sometimes other souls will share the karma, as well. Famous people are also iconic and universal symbols, and as a result many people can learn by observing them and stepping into their shoes. The most important indication of whether you are actually attached to a famous soul is whether or not you are clearing their karma, and once you realize you have to do that difficult task it becomes far less glamorous to be attached to these people! It is one thing to say, "I am the reincarnation of Henry VIII," and another thing to clear his karma. Be careful who you wish to become!

A Seeker creates with intention, and will challenge the self to be continually aware of what they are manifesting with their thoughts. It takes maturity of the soul to be awake enough to understand that one is responsible for how one interprets an event, and that reality is mutable, and determined by the viewer. Two people can witness the same exact event, and come away with a completely different interpretation of the experience. Not only a different interpretation, but they might describe the events differently as well. Even something with a solid third-dimensional reality basis may be seen differently: someone may say that the car that sped by them was blue and large, while another person might say the car was white and small. Memories vary with the people who hold them. Reality is held within the mind of the human who experiences it. Criminal cases are often settled based on evidence that is actually quite circumstantial. Yes, the car was either blue or white, but without a picture, reality is up for grabs!

When humans choose to manifest an event there can be many reasons why. Although these reasons are usually unknown, the soul has its own wisdom that often belies the wants of the surface mind. Sometimes a person may choose to experience something to teach those around them. A child may manifest a chronic and serious illness because the parents need to understand how to care for someone who has long-term dependencies, or they have to learn to love in an unconditional fashion. Someone may choose to become blind or deaf to heighten their ability to use their more subtle senses, and it is a gift they have given themselves. Illness is not a punishment, as the human ego often believes, it is a gift; albeit a more difficult one to accept and process. Human beings learn through their humanness, and their illness, and oftentimes death offers the human race the opportunity to express humility and compassion. When we care for one another we deepen our inter-connectedness, and remember that we are all one, and we must love each other with unconditional grace. When human beings believe that perfection means being perfect, they lose the opportunity to experience grace in all its forms.

So, before you interpret human manifestation as being a simple event which might be expressed as, "You think it and then you get it," you must consider all the energies which are impacting the act of creation. As a Seeker you must begin to understand what motivates you. You must ask yourself some important questions.

**EXERCISE FIVE:** If I am responsible for many of the perimeters of my life, and I chose them before incarnating into this existence, what is the purpose of the choices I made? Examine some of the most significant events in your life from the point of view that you chose them, and ask yourself what could be the reason you made such a choice prior to incarnating. Remember that the soul is responding to the accumulated experiences from many lifetimes, and you can get wedded to being a victim because you are punishing yourself for a past life where you were a perpetrator. Then again you could be teaching others with your experiences and you are definitely teaching yourself.

Take a moment to contemplate some of the events of your life from this newer point of view. Meditate and ask your guides to show you a lifetime where the difficulty started. When the image arises allow it to move forward or backward in time. Begin to guide yourself into and through your past lives as a means to understand your present one.

# Chapter Six

## *The Attack Of The Dark*

*Remember how you have lain on your back in the sun? You lift your hand to block the sun's rays and find your tiny hand can cover the sun and create darkness on your face. The sun is so large, and yet you think your hand has blocked it from your face. Fear is like your hand. Fear blocks the light of God and makes you think it isn't reaching you. But, the fear is so infinitesimal compared to the power of God, that it could never block it. It merely makes you think that you have; just as your hand thinks it has blocked the entire sun. Stand back a little, and you will see your hand in its true proportion. (Given to me by God when I was wrestling with intense fear—Margaret)*

In a Multiverse filled with duality, where there is light there will also be dark. If there is up, there will also be down. Seekers and Starseeds are aware that the Multiverse contains all types of life forms, both seen and unseen. They also know that some of these are friendly, while others are belligerent and mean-spirited. On the Earth, and in the third and fourth dimension, both positive and negative energy exist. Although it may not exist in the same manner for higher dimensional beings (such as angels) as it does on Earth, humans are well aware of both the negative and positive poles.

Most people first ask, when considering negative entities, or energies: "Who is doing this?" Perhaps they do not understand, or want to acknowledge, that there is a force or consciousness of negative energy that opposes the Lightbearers, and those who are doing good work in the world. Perhaps it is also because most people do not believe enough in their personal power, and have handed it over to others time and time again, and so they feel completely helpless when they consider a Family of Dark. As a result they may choose to ignore its influence in the world, which, of course, merely empowers the Family of Dark. The Family of Dark needs the shadows to effectively operate in; light reveals truth and so becomes their enemy. Recognizing the darkness does not make you evil; it means you have the strength, and the light necessary to reveal it. Archangel Michael's ability to venture into dark places, reveal and overcome the darkness is due to the great Light he carries. Strengthening your Light, and your resolve, brings you the courage you will need to stand strong in the face of darkness, and not run away in fear.

I recently asked God, "Why is all this darkness allowed in the world? Not only now, but historically?" I know that darkness challenges us to be strong and keeps us from stasis, but I feel that light and dark have been so out of balance when we look at all the war and pain. He said, *"As long as humanity refuses to recognize the darkness, they will forever be enslaved by it."* That may seem harsh, but I suspect it's true; what we can't recognize we can't fix, and what we fear will always have power over us.

There has always been a debate as to whether *true* evil exists. Some believe in the existence of true evil, while others believe that those who act in an evil manner are merely misguided. Those who desire a more peaceful world, with the "live and let live" point of view, believe that mistaken humans are the ones who force their will upon other people. Some believe that pure evil does exist, meaning that there are those who worship evil and intend to do nothing but evil. Some think those people just need a little more love and understanding. Whatever you accept, you can be sure that living on Earth will present many challenges to your point of view. In fact, your belief systems about evil may change radically because of your experiences.

At one time or another (whether they are aware of it or not) all humans will encounter dark, or negative evil-intentioned energy. Most people would like to ignore those people and energies, and many believe that ignorance is indeed bliss. But, oftentimes a spiritual initiate will encounter these energies or people and if they are not equipped to process or deal with these experiences they flounder in fear.

The story of Buddha and the demon, Mara, his tempter, represents the idea that one must encounter these dark energies, face them, and overcome them in order to be free of them. Many supernatural creatures are found in Buddhist literature; Mara is often called the Lord of Death. First Mara tempts Siddhartha Gautama (Buddha) to weaken his resolve and lead him into the darker/shadow self. But, Siddhartha Gautama overcomes his fear of the dark, even when Mara sends vast armies of demons and monsters to attack him. Siddhartha says, "I bear you witness!" to Mara, and Mara disappears. In this mythology it is said that the next morning Siddhartha achieves enlightenment. Notice that in this story he did not achieve enlightenment until he could "bear it witness," or recognize the demons. The spiritual initiate realizes that freedom is achieved by facing the darkness, not by denying it. This is exactly what God meant when he told me, "As long as humanity refuses to recognize the darkness, they will forever be enslaved by it." I suspect God was talking about both the darkness outside, and inside ourselves.

Nichiren Daishonin, a Buddhist monk who lived in thirteenth century Japan states, "Good and evil have been inherent in life since time without beginning, and they remain in one's life through all the stages of the Bodhisattva practice up to the stage of near-perfect enlightenment."

The temptation of Jesus by the devil is well known. After being baptized, Jesus fasted for forty days and nights and during this time the devil appeared to Jesus and tempted him. Only by facing the devil and refusing the temptations could he become free of his ego; it is then that the angels bring him nourishment.

The Hindu religion has categorized many types of demons. Some of these include: Pishacha (carnivorous demons), Vetala (vampires who live in dead bodies), Vinayakas (demons who create obstacles), just to name a few.

Merlin has wrestled with his version of Satan for many, many thousands and thousands of years, and he understands that a human cannot escape encountering darkness. A Seeker understands that where there is a Family of Light, there must also be a Family of Dark; for light always casts a shadow. Modern psychology is uncomfortable with the idea of evil energy, but those who have experienced an encounter with it cannot deny its existence; just as those who have seen an angel of Light and Love must accept its existence as fact.

By the time a Seeker has completed all their earthly incarnations they have come to understand the existence of evil, and its place in creation. From the point of view of your Higher Self, the experience of duality is one of the greatest gifts the Earth plane gives an individual. You know light when you know dark and you know dark when you know light. If God is All That Is, then all of it is within God and serves a purpose. No matter what path we take we are learning and growing.

You can believe that angelic beings have experienced evil, if you believe that the battle that began in heaven has landed on Earth; however, as they are not in a physical form, their perception of evil is quite different from ours. The density of the third dimension has its own challenges. Seekers are well aware of the fact that one of the lessons they will gain through their incarnations into the density of the third dimension, is the opportunity to experience separation. During their many cycles of reincarnation humans will experience the existence of evil from both the third and the fourth dimension. The third dimensional challenges are well known: bullying, fascism, enslavement, murder, rape, lying, betrayal, cheating and stealing are merely a few of the physical expressions of evil. These experiences disempower the victim, and energetically feed the perpetrator. Many perpetrators will say that while they are harming another they feel high and more powerful.

During their lifetime there are many people who experience these extreme expressions of evil, and there are those who spend their entire life surrounded by this type of behavior. In fact, there are many people who doubt the existence of good; and certainly given their life experiences they can make a case for it. But, anyone with a balanced perspective understands that both good and evil exist on the planet

Earth, and most people have the potential to express both of these as well.

Seekers are particularly interested in understanding human behavior and because of this they will encounter extreme expressions of both good and evil during their many lifetimes. They will study human behavior because they realize that human beings on the Earth are emotionally the most complex life forms they will encounter anywhere throughout the galaxies. Because human beings have been given free will, and a strong and powerful ego center, they are most interesting to study and observe. Although this may be a shocking idea to many, it is important to understand that humans are studied and observed by a wide variety of beings from many dimensions. Many of you have encountered interactions with these multidimensional beings, and have been afraid to speak of these events. Well, now you can. If the human race is to evolve it is important that those who understand levels of reality beyond the three dimensions speak up.

The biggest difference between a Seeker and a non-Seeker is that a Seeker will consider humanity from the outside. What does that mean? It means that they will often observe humanity as though they are outsiders, and many times feel that they exist outside of the human race in some manner. If you have identified yourself as a Starseed, but you are not a typical Seeker, these feelings of being an outsider may also apply to you as well. Remember that Seekers are Starseeds, but not all Starseeds are Seekers. Starseeds are human beings who clearly remember having incarnated on other planets.

How does evil impact the typical Seeker and Starseed? Those of you who remember your past lives know you have suffered during numerous lifetimes; often at the hands of those who wished to silence you. If you are a Starseed you may remember having faced evil on other planets as well as on Earth. If you have faced evil over and over, you may have also recognized that you have been a perpetrator of evil deeds. You may realize that there were times either in this life, or in other lifetimes, when your anger and rage pushed you to commit a crime and create karma. Although Seekers are fascinated by human motivation, and will strive to understand what influences can turn a good person bad, they also ask, "What is it that separates someone who creates evil, because their emotional wounding pushes them to it, from someone who worships evil and plots and plans how to bring more evil into the world?" It is intention.

The definition of evil, for this book, will be someone (or something) who intends to create pain and suffering for others. It means that their intention is to do harm, and to drain the human's power. Now we will turn our focus toward energies and entities that exist multi-dimensionally, in other words, the beings that can impact the world while both seen and unseen.

The first and most important thing to understand is that while humans (for all intents and purposes) are trapped in third-dimensional density, these beings are not. Although they can be more comfortable taking shape in the fourth dimensional realm, it is possible for them to come through portals, or doorways, into the third dimension and impact humans on the physical plane. Most humans consciously encounter the fourth dimension only when they dream, and it is during nightmares that they encounter demonic and ill-intentioned energies. The portals that the demonic uses to enter the human world are emotionally based, and the entity attaches to humans and impacts them through their emotional fields.

From the perspective of a fourth-dimensional entity, human emotion is like food, and they are the parasites that feed from the energy released by the individual emotions. For example, different addictions attract different demonic energies, and an alcoholic is attracting and expressing different energy than a crack addict, a heroin addict, a sex addict or a nicotine addict. Sometimes these parasitic energies will include Lost Souls. Lost Souls are essentially humans who had the same problem while alive and now, after death, feed on others who have the same issues. These Lost Souls exist in the fourth dimension, and need the human host to continue the addiction so they can feed. Demonic beings are not human, and they do not understand or comprehend the world as a human does. They make their choices on where to feed from an energetic perspective. They can be directed to attack by someone, but they will only stay around the energetic field of a person if they can find something to hook onto. You can imagine if that wasn't true then every human would be covered with these parasites.

It is important to recognize that when these demonic vermin attach they will impact the emotional body of the human host. The human will feel hopeless, drained, suicidal and depressed, or if they are attached onto by a violent entity, they will be murderous and chaotic. Sometimes, the human will find it almost impossible to lift themselves above the lower frequencies these vampires need, and the condition becomes a vicious cycle where the human feels depressed and vulnerable, attracts the energy, and then cannot release themselves from it because the entity is increasing the negative emotions. These energies benefit from the fact that most humans do not recognize their existence, and so they can live freely without fear of being found out. If you doubt their existence, then you haven't worked in a rehab unit or the prison system. If you wonder if they are getting more effective, then you haven't heard the statistics on addiction and the prison systems, or the number of teenagers now addicted to heroin. Addiction attracts dark energy, and you will never be free of the dark energy until you are free of the addiction. They go hand-in-hand.

Most Starseeds, Seekers and Lightbearers have experienced psychic attacks, and they have wondered what these attackers are and how to protect themselves from these attacks. I have been asked about this issue many times over the years. Why are they targeted? Who is targeting them? These are valid questions. Here are some of the main reasons these beings will attack or attach:

1. Because the host supplies emotional fear-based nourishment for the attacker.

2. Because the host is bringing Light to the world, and the dark entity views them as a threat. Depending on how much light is brought, and the mission of the Lightbearer, this will determine the nature and type of the attack.

3. The person suffering the attack has a karmic debt or past life attachment to the dark entity. For example, if someone was a dark witch or wizard in a past life, and they brought evil energies through portals, and then betrayed them, they could be attacked by them over and over again. If someone is conjuring dark energy in this life the energy can also turn on them, and attack them. Dark demons are unstable, and will feed anywhere.

4. A long-standing family curse can be carried through generation to generation. Or a curse can be put on by an unscrupulous psychic. *(A client of mine had a curse put on her by a psychic in NYC who threatened her with a curse if she didn't pay three thousand dollars! The client didn't pay. When the curse was released, she saw black smoke rising from her body.)*

5. Someone is exploring metaphysical or physical realms and revealing information that might weaken the Family of Dark if it is revealed. Whistleblowers fall into this category as well. These are some of the reasons psychic attacks might happen. Each category varies in its complexity. There are certainly many subcategories within the categories.

As strange as it may seem, the dark energy cannot attach to your body permanently without some type of karmic agreement. Even when they want to break the karmic tie to the entity, the person who is hosting the entity might become so weak, because of the parasitic nature of the attachment, that they might find it difficult to gain enough strength to counteract the force of the entity. In these cases, a healer who can assist to free the human from the attachment can be quite helpful. Fear can act as an invitation to the energy because it weakens the aura and lessens the life force. But, the energy can't get in and stay attached to you, if you do not attract it in some way. It need not be a conscious attraction, however.

*(Too many clients I have seen over the years have admitted to actually giving these demonic/ dark beings permission to enter their body, and are now plagued by them. For example, they will say, "I was lonely," or "The entity just kept bugging me over and over so I said, yes." Your best*

*defense is to deny. Never say yes to them when they try to seduce, or force their way into your life, body or home. Remember that Mara tempted Siddhartha, but he refused.)*

These dark energies will often need to weaken you to enter your aura as well. This is often accomplished emotionally. If they can't get to you directly, then they can get to you through others. Emotions can be manipulated easily in your friends and family members: betrayal, abandonment, poverty, jealousy, envy, guilt, all of these can be used to create chaos and weaken the intended victim. Once the emotional damage has been dealt, the energy can find an entry-way. This is one reason it is so important to do your emotional work. Being strong and clear, awake and aware is your best defense!

To understand who is doing the attacking it is important to explain who some of these beings are:

**Vampires:** Yes. They are real. They come in two forms: Energetic and Physical. Of course, a vampire is a vampire, and the definition is the same: a parasitic entity that drains the life force from another entity. The first question you may ask yourself is, "Why?" These beings will attack and drain other beings because they are incapable of receiving energy from the God-Source. Because they cannot feed themselves energetically from Love and Light they must receive nourishment from other humans. Yes, your aunt Brunhilda can be a vampire if she continually drains you by weakening you with insults or passive-aggressive behavior. These human-energy vampires are easy to avoid and recognize. Stand your ground and eventually they move on to someone who agrees to feed them by playing their "control-drama" games.

**Demons:** Demons enter the Earth through energetic portals; they are multidimensional energies. On the Earth they exist primarily on the fourth dimension. There are numerous demons. They infect the brain of the human and host inside it. They can alter the personality and even take over the human completely. This is most commonly known as a possession. None of the demonic subspecies know how to receive energy from light so they need you to be their food source, or battery charger. Because they need an energetic match to host on, they too are energetic parasites.

**Lost Souls**: These are human ghosts and poltergeists that exist in the fourth dimension, and cannot move on because they are obsessed with the Earth plane. This can be because of unfinished business, or they just don't know how to move on to higher realms. A ghost can be very benign, such as your Aunt Martha. These benign or friendly beings are *not* Lost Souls. A Lost Soul forgets their connection to the Divine, and if they are stuck in that state for a long time they can become agitated and aggressive. To move them on is possible, but this can be more difficult to do than just suggesting they "Go to the Light." If you encounter a truly Lost Soul ghost it is best to offer them what they need in terms of forgiveness or solace. You must honor their free will, as these are human souls, and you cannot force them to go anywhere. *(Tips on moving a Lost Soul are in Chapter Eleven: Death and Dying.)*

**Devils**: These are demons that have developed a consciousness that is evolved enough to have a game-plan that is actually quite sophisticated. They not only feed off of Lost Souls, but will try to destroy humans who interfere with their intentions. They often guard large portals and feed off the Lost Souls trapped within these portals.

These are some of the most common psychic and physical attackers that plague human beings. Now, what can you do to protect yourself? The most important thing seems the most simple. Do your personal homework and release your ego desires and your fears. They need your fear and ego to manipulate you. The Buddha taught non-attachment because when you are not attached to your ego's needs and wants they cannot attach to you.

Jesus was a master exorcist and cast out demons regularly:

> *From* the *New American Standard Bible, Matthew 8:28-34:*
>
> *"When He came to the other side into the country of Gadarenes, two men who were demon-possessed met Him as they were coming out of the tombs. They were so extremely violent that no*

*one could pass by that way. And they cried out, saying 'What business do we have with each other, Son of God? Have You come here to torment us before the time? . . . The demons began to entreat Him, saying, 'If You are going to cast us out, send us into the herd of swine.' And He said to them, 'Go!' and they came out and went into the swine . . . ."*

If you are being plagued by psychic attack it would behoove you to try calling on Jesus, regardless of your religious beliefs. Jesus will respond when called on for this task. What he taught is the use of higher energy (which is really the frequency of unconditional love) to be rid of these beings; they hate the vibration of pure unconditional love and will flee it. Both of these Masters knew that they had to wrestle with these beings: Buddha with Mara and Jesus with the Devil. They were not free of the struggle by any means.

As mentioned in the previous chapter, Archangel Michael is also a powerful energy to assist humans to clear these dark energies. Call on Archangel Michael to protect you with his sword, light-shield and Legion of Angels. They will respond.

**EXERCISE SIX**: If you have been taught that if you are on the path of enlightenment it means you are above the struggle with dark energies you will need to rethink this. If Buddha and Jesus wrestled with the lower forces during their lifetime it stands to reason that you will as well. How did they free themselves? As a Seeker it is your job to ask yourself these questions, and also to discover the answer. You can receive assistance, but it will be your job to run into and not away from these issues. Exercise Six requires your complete honesty with your fears. What are you afraid of? Where does your ego lead you astray? Knowing your trigger buttons is essential to protecting yourself. Fear and unresolved issues are enormous triggers that can set any human into a tail-spin and cause them to act from their lower self. People attack when they are afraid and threatened, and mastery requires honesty with the self. Why have you been triggered into a fear response? Why are you reacting the way you are? Are you acting from love or fear?

At the other end of the spectrum, do you try and rescue every person like they were a stray dog? It stands to reason then, that you are going to be letting in negative energies, because you are not protecting yourself. If you are opening your life, and energy field, to any person that needs to feed off of others, you will become a victim. Be honest and look at how you invite these energies into your life.

Protecting yourself is also addressed in a later chapter; however, you must meet your fears head-on before you jump ahead. Do some channeled writing on these questions and see what your Higher Self or guides have to say on the issue. More than likely they will tell you that the mind must be free of fear for the heart center to be activated. Freedom is achieved when the heart and mind are in balance.

# Chapter Seven

## *The Fall From Eden—Karmic Imprints Of The Starseeds*

If you believe that God is All That Is, then it stands to reason that the One cannot be separated from itself, and all humans, and all beings throughout this Multiverse are involved in a reality that began as far back as reality itself. The first creational realms, the fall of the angels into density, and the subsequent battles for power and domination created by these beings, spread out throughout time and space to consume all of creation. Some have dubbed this battle the Orion Wars, but in fact, although the Orion Wars reflect the battle, it began even before the Wars themselves, and it began when angels first incarnated into Dragons, and ushered in the creational/dimensional realms.

Many people who research and delve deeply into the Extra-terrestrial phenomenon call them Inter-dimensional beings; not Extra-terrestrial. However, it is my contention that the two are not exclusive and these beings are and can be both. Our human mind wants to categorize them as one *or* the other. Why, in fact can't they be both? It is also true that many people want to make them all good or all bad. Once again, why should they be relegated to something so simple? Humanity is certainly neither one nor the other, and our ability to perceive these beings, not as one thing, but numerous things will draw us closer to truth. The child-mind in us wants to make it easy and clear-cut, but the adult in us knows that reality is rarely, if ever, so.

The intergalactic Orion Wars (the memories of which so many of you are beginning to access) are essentially fueled by the desire of those who cannot acquire knowledge directly from the Source. These vampires conquer and steal the knowledge of those who can. By "access knowledge directly," it is meant: through Light from Source. Because the dark cannot access knowledge through Light, they conquer and enslave those who can. Memories such as being on a "Blue Planet" and holding knowledge in the belly, or a "Purple Planet" and holding knowledge of sacred geometry and mathematics, are awakening in vast numbers of Starseeds.

*(Recently a client of mine remembered being on an "Orange Planet" and being attacked by an enormous black Dragon-like being.)*

Many also remember being invaded by creatures that appear to be robots, Reptilians, spiders, and other fierce and unfeeling manifestations that eviscerate and destroy the knowledge-keepers, and steal the wisdom held within the individual, and the planet as a whole. These memories awaken simultaneously with the awakening of the Earth human that you are today; it is the integration of the self.

This book is far from a scientific manual, and is interested not in scientific theories, but instead, how the experiences held within the memory banks of the soul impact the human you are today. These memories cannot be denied, as they are arising separately from people's consciousness all over the world.

*(Some of the famous books from those working with the extra-terrestrials include: "We the Arcturians," by Dr. Norma J. Milanovich, "Bringers of the Dawn," by Barbara Marciniak, and "No More Secrets, No More Lies," by Patricia Cori.)*

Earth became a melting pot for many of the displaced Starseeds from these wars. The biblical *Book of Enoch* discusses the Nephilim, or children, half-angel and half-human, who populated the Earth, and dominated the less-evolved humans. The story is millennia old, and so quite complex, but in order to simplify it, and to help the reader to understand where they might play a part in this history, this chapter defines some of the struggles of the various Starseeds, and helps them to recognize how those stories are still with them today. Chapter Nine will investigate the Nephilim themselves and clarify the Dragon/angel/human/Reptilian connection.

Your karma goes where you go. You cannot escape your soul; nor should you want to. Your soul (and spirit) is connected to all your experiences, and from the point of view of your soul all your lifetimes are a single lifetime done in multiple bodies, and that includes the lives you have lived off the Earth, and on other planets. That means that you cannot separate yourself from your karma, you cannot run away from it, and you will be required to heal it, and integrate it, no matter how good or bad it is. Everywhere you go, there you are, which makes the healing of your spirit even more important.

It is important to realize that your soul is not confined to one Starseed imprint alone. If you are an Ancient One, meaning you have been incarnating for many eons, more than likely you have experienced so many different bodies, and Star Systems, that it would be impossible to name them all. However, most Starseeds, even those who have had multiple incarnations, will find that they resonate more strongly with one or another Star System. You may have had a life as a Praying Mantis being (yes they exist and are about 7 feet tall!), but you may not be carrying that imprint strongly in your field. You may not be dealing with karma from that Star System.

The deepest wounding to the soul occurred when you "fell out of Eden" the first time. Being pushed out of the nest (in many cases quite harshly) created a karmic complex, and mental mantra, that you have carried with you ever since. In this chapter we will explore some of the more common complexes, and where they arose, and offer up some possibilities for healing those challenging complexes.

Each Starseed carries a complex that is deeply buried, but drives their current and past lives in profound ways. Although there are universal issues we all suffer from (and we all suffer from all of these in some manner) the complexes will be more deeply etched within some of us than others. Whether you are an Ancient One, who remembers the fall from the angelic realm into the body of a Dragon, or you remember being Pleiadian, Arcturian or any other Starseed, this chapter will shed light on some of the typical emotional wounding these Starseeds carry. *(There are many people today who are beginning to explore their extra-terrestrial roots; they may have a very different experience than is listed here. There is room for all of us to express our understanding about this complex topic! This is my experience, and my client's experiences, but we are only in the beginning stages of awakening our ET stories, and no one claims to know it all!)*

When the Orion Wars were in full swing, the Draconian armies invaded many planetary systems with the desire to capture, utilize, or destroy the native species, depending on which of these paths served their needs. The Draconian armies are not one species; instead they are a complex military assemblage made up of many different organic and inorganic beings. Knowing where you were at the time of the original invasion of your planet can define your complex, and assist you to understand yourself more fully. Listed below are some typical experiences for some of the Starseeds; notice which ones resonate most deeply for you. My clients' memories are contained in these descriptions.

**Arcturians:** The Arcturians are currently highly evolved spiritual beings who hold consciousness in the fifth and sixth dimensions. During the Orion Wars, unlike many of the other planetary systems, the Arcturians knew that the invaders were coming, and prepared themselves to meet the onslaught by moving out of the third and fourth dimensional lower astral realms, where they knew they would be seen, to higher dimensional realms (fifth and sixth) where they knew they could not be captured. To understand this energetic shift from the human point of view is to understand that the angels exist alongside us, but in a higher dimensional realm, which we cannot (usually) see or reach. That dimensional barrier keeps them safe from lower dimensional contamination, and this is the same idea with the Arcturians. Although they do not vibrate at the same level as an Archangel, they currently vibrate high enough to avoid detection by lower life forms and entities.

When the Arcturians were in danger of being attacked, they protected themselves by enacting this vibrational lift, and those who could not hold the higher consciousness frequencies, and might endanger the majority of the people, were cast-off into space to fend for the self. Most often the Arcturian was quarantined by a vibrational separation. This means that those who could not sustain a high vibration, and might endanger the entire planet, by lowering its frequency, were lined up and cast off into space.

*(Some of you might be reminded of the ideas that were circulated around the Mayan Calendar, December 21, 2012 event. Some believed that the planet would ascend into a fifth dimensional frequency at that time, and those who could not vibrate high enough would be left behind. One could certainly surmise that perhaps this was stimulated by the old memory of the Arcturian experience.)*

The journey of the Arcturian who did not make the jump into a higher frequency is an individual one. There is no one single path that took place after being cast-off, but in the search for a new home many Arcturian souls eventually settled on Earth. Earth is a mish-mosh of galactic beings, and they felt that they would be accepted on this planet. However, like so many Starseeds, human-Arcturians will feel that the Earth is not their true home.

A group of Arcturians did not take human bodies and enter the human soul progression upon leaving Arcturus and landing on Earth. These are the Gray Aliens that are talked about in various books and movies; they are the ones with the large eyes and bulging heads. The Arcturians and the Grays look very much alike, but the Gray Aliens are the unevolved, lower-vibrational expression of the Arcturians. Some of these Grays were captured by the Draconian Reptilians and utilized as a part of their army. Some arrived on Earth, but never took human form. They are creating a hybrid human race which mingles the Arcturian Gray DNA with the human DNA and they are also involved in many of the abductions and subsequent experimentation that has taken place. If you or a loved one has been visited by, or worked with, these individuals you can be certain that you have a karmic tie to them that stems from the Orion Wars. If you are afraid of them it is also important to delve into your past life, galactic karma, so that you can heal those karmic cords.

*(This is what Dr. Norma J. Milanovich says about the advanced Arcturians in her book, We the Arcturians. "They are the most loving and non-judgmental beings you can imagine. Their skin is a greenish color. They have very large, almond-shaped eyes. They have only three fingers. They have the ability to move objects with their minds and are totally telepathic. Their source of nourishment is an effervescent liquid that is highly vitalizing to their entire being.")*

The human-incarnated Arcturian Elders, who enacted the quarantine, and made the decision to separate the Arcturian community by vibration, often carry the karmic guilt of this decision. Prior to the quarantine the community had been very unified, and closed, (by human standards) and the welfare of all Arcturians was the consideration of all others. Now, faced with destruction they had to make a decision to save some of their people or perhaps all would perish. It was a difficult decision for the Elders whose job it was to enact the separation. Some families were ripped apart. Others remember being lined up, and then sent away.

Those who were booted-off, often repeat the story in their human dramas lifetime after lifetime. They are always searching for a community to welcome them, and they often struggle with feelings of being unworthy or less than others. Arcturian-humans tend to be asexual, or not very interested in lower vibrational expressions of sex; they may enjoy the closeness it brings, but feel perfectly happy to live a life with little, or even no sexual expression. Many Arcturian-humans (especially the Elders) will have lives in monasteries, ashrams, convents and other spiritually-based communities.

Humans who are incarnated Arcturian Elders can appear very aloof, and carry the air of being above others. They tend to dislike looking at the shadow side of humanity (and themselves) because it uncomfortably reminds their unconscious of how they pushed away the lower vibrational members of their society. To heal their karma they must be willing to get their hands dirty on Earth by compassionately assisting people to lift their vibration. They must curb their arrogance and tendency toward cold-heartedness, and allow themselves to experience, without judgment, the human emotional range.

Those who connect easily with the Arcturian Motherships are also working with the higher-vibrational Arcturians to heal the ancient karma, and give all Arcturians the opportunity to come home again.

The longing for the Arcturian soul often revolves around the need for community, and because of this many Arcturians are attracted to religious and spiritual communities where they can live and worship on Earth. These places often make them feel they have "come home" again. If the Arcturian was booted off they can give up their power too easily to someone they consider to be spiritually superior to them, and if they are accepted it proves to them that they were worthy after all. If they have put their faith in someone they feel betrays that faith, then they may feel more abandoned than ever, and become embittered or disillusioned. The lesson is to trust the self, and release the need to be accepted by others to feel worthy.

The human-incarnated Arcturian Elders must release their belief that they are superior, and be willing to acknowledge the reality around them. They must admit that they are on a planet of duality which contains both good and evil, dark and light, and rather than ignore or rush to fix everyone or everything because they know best, they must learn to surrender, and watch, without the need to do something. Earth provides the opportunity to learn from a massive range of experiences, and learning to honor many different paths is the task of the Arcturian Elder who has chosen to incarnate upon Earth. To heal the ancient karma one must first be willing to look at the self, and understand where your insecurities lie. The healing involves not pushing away the darkness, and the shadow, but embracing all pieces of the self and others. It means truly being non-judgmental.

The Arcturian Motherships exist above the Earth in a fifth and sixth dimensional (and even higher) vibrational field. Those aboard the ships feel some responsibility for life on Earth because so many of their people are currently incarnated here. They watch over the Earthlings, and gladly assist when asked. It is especially useful to call on high-vibrational Arcturians for assistance in healing as they are excellent healers.

*(The first time I met an Arcturian-human was many years ago, long before I was aware of the various Starseeds. I was at a party and felt compelled to ask a man, "Are you an angel?" He answered, "No, I'm an Arcturian," and then he suggested I read the book, "We the Arcturians.")*

**Pleiadians**: The Pleiadians have a very complex soul history. Like their fellow Starseeds from Lyra, some of them left the Pleiades after it was attacked and hid out in the fairy realm on Earth. But, this is not true for all of them by any means, and they can be difficult to categorize. Whereas human-Arcturians will be drawn to spiritual communities which encourage sameness among the members, Pleiadian-humans will most often be drawn to lives of artistic expression, beauty, the need to stand-out among their peers with self-expression and individuation. Pleiadians make wonderful artists, (singers, dancers, actors, painters) anything that allows them to express themselves. Because on their home plane, prior to the invasion, they lived a idyllic existence which gave them the opportunity to play with energy and create as they desired, it is common for Pleiadians on Earth to long for a similar type of existence. They are often sensitive, and it is difficult for them to accept the harshness of Earth.

Like Arcturians they may be drawn to spiritual communities, but they will also need to maintain some individual expression and will continue their work as artists and artisans within the community. They often work with crystals to heal and beautify their home environment. Unlike the majority of human-Arcturians, Pleiadians are sensualists and usually will enjoy sex as a creative expression. Pleiadians connect to Mother Earth and they will draw strength from trees, flowers, plants, crystals and animals. They are the classic tree-huggers.

Some of the Pleiadian planets used individuals who were able to vibrate at a frequency beyond the rest of the society; these beings acted as Queen Bees to keep the vibration of their planet high and create a fifth, sixth and seventh dimensional world for the others to enjoy. These beings acted like transmitting towers, using their bodies to send out high-vibration energy.

You might ask, "Why, if they vibrated at the fifth, sixth and seventh dimension were they captured by the lower vibration Draconians? If the Arcturians escaped by raising their collective vibration to that place, why didn't it work for the Pleiadians?" The answer is that when news of the Orion Wars reached the ears of the Pleiadian Queen Bees they began to experience fear, which lowered their vibrational energy. Prior to that point the Pleiades was literally off the radar to the Draconian Reptilian invaders. Once again think of how beings such as angels on other dimensions can't be seen by humans because they vibrate too high. Fear, however, lowers the vibration of an energy field, and when the fear began to infect the Pleiadian Queen Bees, the signals they sent out lowered as well.

When the Pleiadians were invaded by the Draconian Reptilians they were either used as slaves, killed, or they were captured, and studied or experimented on, for their abilities. Some were also mated with, and a Pleiadian-Reptilian hybrid was created. The Pleiadian-Rptilian karma is rampant today. For example, many artists with Pleaidian creative energy are managed by Reptilian "masters." Many Pleiadians will have Reptilian boyfriends, mothers, fathers and so forth. This is because of the karma that they hold with these individuals; it is their job in this life to step from fear, and get their personal power back from these Reptilian-humans.

Pleiadian-humans who remember this invasion report that it was swift and brutal. This fear is repeated by human-Pleiadians today in this manner: they often will say to others, "Don't talk about the dark stuff, or you'll draw it to you." They will run away from people who talk about the darker side of reality because they fear it will lower their vibration, and they will be attacked by it. If you know someone who does this to you, or if you do this, it is very likely you are dealing with a Pleiadian karmic imprint. Learning to keep your vibration high in the presence of darkness is the maturing of the Pleiadian-human soul.

The Pleiadian Queen Bees often want to be responsible for holding up the vibration of a group, but they must learn to let go of the ancient task, and realize that their job is instead to make everyone hold their own vibration. The responsibility for holding one's vibration high is the job of the individual. In other words, each person must rescue themselves. Co-dependency creates weakness and self-responsibility strengthens the individual.

When the Pleiadians were attacked they were like innocent children on a playground who were suddenly invaded by evil. The Pleiadians did not even have a word for evil (or a thought to contain the presence of evil in their midst) and at first they were merely confused at the sudden appearance of the Draconian Reptilian soldiers. They soon discovered that something quite new and awful was happening to them.

The Pleiadian Queen Bees were captured and utilized through DNA experimentation and interbreeding. Because they were highly evolved and gifted, the Reptilians did not kill them but kept them as prisoners of war. This karma on Earth has been repeated over and over. Human-Reptilians and human-Pleiadians have been recreating their karma back and forth for many lifetimes. On Earth, when the Pleiadians have expressed their psychic gifts and abilities, they have often been tortured as witches. This has left them fearful, angry, wary or in denial if they are running fast and hard enough from their fear.

Human-Pleiadians are often involved in painful karma with a Reptilian parent, spouse, or even child. If they have become wedded to victim status through many lifetimes they could be unwilling to free themselves from the bond, and if they are ready to be free and take back their personal power, they will struggle to cut the ties that bind. However, upon doing the karmic cord release they will feel lighter, and freer than they have in many lifetimes.

How does a Pleiadian-human heal and become released from fear? First and most importantly for the soul journey is to realize that you are on the Earth to learn to hold your vibration high in midst of lower density. Maturity happens on Earth through overcoming odds, strengthening resolve in the face of struggle, and learning to love with eyes wide open to reality, not by denying it or running away from it. The sooner a Pleiadian-human can strengthen their intention to face fear with bravery, not escapism of any kind, the sooner they will have understood the gifts of being an Earth-human.

*(One of my Pleiadian Queen Bee clients expressed how she was with money. "Sometimes I feel like I have millions of dollars and imagine myself buying a multi-million dollar estate, and the next minute I realize I only have $100 in my checking account, and I'm in fear of poverty! Why is that, and how can I change it?" The angels explained to her that energetically as a Queen Bee she was able to draw and anchor in enormous amounts of Creative God Force; with the help of other Queen Bees, she could supply spiritual energy to the entire planet. When she failed to maintain that, and was cast into fear during the Orion Wars, she went instantly into energetic darkness. The teetering back and forth between being overly-abundant, and poverty-stricken, is the replaying of her old Pleiadian karmic pattern. Money represents creative God-Force energy, and when she feels super-abundant, it suddenly triggers her old wounding, and she falls into the old experience of energetic poverty. To balance this she must first be aware of it, and then find a mid-way point; notice what amount of money and energy she can hold comfortably, and balance what she receives with what she gives out, energetically.)*

*(Those of you interested in reading books written by a Pleiadian channel might want to begin with the Barbara Marciniak books. Also, Barbara Hand Clow's, The Pleiadian Agenda: A New Cosmology for the Age of Light, is only one of the many books she has published from a Pleiadian perspective.)*

**Sirians (from the Sirius Star System) and the Annunaki**: The human-Sirians and the human-Annunaki, just like other Starseeds, have their Orion Wars story. It is important to remember that Earth is currently (at the time of writing this) in the middle of the Orion Wars, even though few humans are aware of this.

Again, all of the karma that has been created throughout the many galaxies has arrived on the Earth for us to heal. No wonder life as a human is challenging and overwhelming! The typical Sirian-human is powerful; but many of them are in hiding. Having misused their power terribly in previous lifetimes, not only do they not admit to others how powerful they are, they often feel overwhelmed by their karma and surprisingly powerless.

The term, Annunaki, in modern times has become a catch-phrase for the Sumarian gods, the Illuminati, and the royal Reptilian bloodlines said to rule this planet. The idea of the Annunaki, as presented by Zecharia Sitchin, as extraterrestrial beings, has influenced modern thought in this area profoundly. Author of many books, he popularized the information of the planetary body called Nibiru, which he claimed was located beyond Pluto. So, the term Annunaki is open to numerous possibilities for definition. In this book the term Annunaki is utilized to express those extraterrestrial gods who came from the Sirius Star System.

It is my belief that we are just beginning to piece together this complex history, and its impact on humanity. If you think about how little we know about our own Earth history, it makes sense that we are still in infancy when it comes to putting the pieces of our galactic history into the puzzle. As humanity begins to awaken to the understanding that there are millions, billions and even trillions of stars out there, and we are only one tiny planet in the midst of it all; they awaken to the knowledge that we are not alone.

Most human-Sirians will be attracted to gemstones and love to wear large pieces of jewelry on their bodies and (if it was a different era) in their hair or in headpieces; but long ago these were not used merely for show. The Sirian-humans understood that these stones carried energy that could be utilized and manipulated to enhance their own power. The elaborate headgear of the Egyptian royalty is a perfect expression of the Sirian soul. Sirian royalty understood how to communicate with extraterrestrials and utilized many different devices to send messages to the Motherships. They also knew how to communicate with beings that dwelt in other dimensions, including the dead. In Egypt only the Starseed royalty were allowed access to the spiritual devices and power structures, and these were carefully guarded, along with the secrets kept in them.

Those of the Sirian-Annunaki lineage are the wizards written about in books, and as most people know, wizards can be dark or light, but they all hold a great deal of power. The Annunaki (Sirian royalty) had not forgotten their wizard tricks when they landed on Earth, and they continually expressed the powers they had on their home planet.

*(During a past life session, one of my clients recalled having the ability to take electricity from the air and direct it through her fingertips. She recalled having the ability to direct the electricity into rock formations that resembled Stonehenge. The ability appeared to activate the stone formations. This mirrors the abilities of the PK MAN, a true story, by Jeffrey Mishlove, PH.D.)*

Tales of Atlantis and the misuse of metaphysical knowledge are directly tied to the Sirian/Annunaki lineage. Most Starseeds will have vivid memories of lives during the time of Atlantis. Many will remember how they, in some manner, either contributed to its fall, or struggled to prevent it. The karma is alive today, as many Starseeds have returned at this time to once again try and stop the self-destruction that hangs over the human race and heal the Atlantean karma.

Because Sirian/Annunaki/humans held a great deal of power, they often suffer karma directly associated with power, and the misuse of power, both physical and metaphysical. Like other Starseeds it is common for those from Sirius to run away from their karma because it is too painful to recognize. Many Sirians, who held positions of tremendous power in past lives, are actually in hiding, and have masked themselves so that others will not recognize them. Although most humans think that if you have been a pharaoh or king in another life you will be a powerful individual in the modern day, very often this is not the truth.

*(The first time, years ago, I worked with such an individual he came in to see me unmasked. He had the enormous, elongated skull of the Annunaki and he radiated power that I had not previously experienced. It frightened me at the time to encounter such an individual. I cannot explain it to you; I don't know what happened, but the second time he came to do past life therapy with me, he was masked, and appeared*

*completely different and looked like a normal human. This Annunaki-human had been a very powerful Egyptian pharaoh in another life. But, in this life was seeking to heal his karmic cords.)*

Because their karma involves the misuse of power, these individuals will often shy away from powerful lives, and instead attempt to heal their karma in quiet service to mankind. It is important for many of these individuals to reclaim their power and speak up by sharing with humanity the gifts and knowledge they have so long repressed. Once they trust themselves to have authority, without abusing it, many of these individuals will once again take up positions of power. To face their karma they must be brave enough to step into the shoes of their past life personalities, and heal the abuses they created. It is also important for them to recognize that the evolutionary history of humanity is intimately intertwined with them, and that they brought a tremendous amount of information, wisdom and growth to the human race. In other words it isn't all bad! The libraries and halls of learning are directly linked to the knowledge of the Sirian Starseeds and without them the human race might still be in the Stone Age, or at least in the Bronze Age.

The idea of a round table, where each member of the council holds power, is actually a Sirian creation and comes directly from the manner of ruling there. Each council member would take a position of leadership and it would rotate among the members. The idea of a just and noble rulership as expressed by the Knights of the Round Table heralds directly from the Sirius Star System. Those attracted to the Arthurian energies often have roots in Sirius.

In West Africa the tribe of the Dogon people spoke about a race of people from the Sirius system called the Nommos. They visited Earth thousands of years ago and resembled the mermaids and mermen. These mermaid beings are depicted on temples, and in art of many traditions. Even Isis is sometimes depicted as a mermaid, to link her to the Sirius Star System.

*(My personal experience has included healing a mermaid who was having serious health issues; when given energetic healing she would*

*immediately return to her mermaid state and enter an altered state of consciousness. I truly believe in the existence of mermaids and mermen. Those who have a link to this mermaid race often connect deeply to the dolphins and whales of today.)*

The Dogons also knew about the triune Sirius Star System; they knew that the planet Jupiter has four major moons, and that Saturn has rings, and that the planets orbit the sun. They knew this long before Galileo and the invention of the telescope. They explained that the beings from Sirius told them this information.

The word Annunaki has become corrupted as many people have written about the abuses of these Sirians, but the Annunaki are not merely evil. Like all other Starseeds they have their strengths and their weaknesses. And, like other humans and Starseeds they are evolving here on planet Earth.

*(No More Secrets, No More Lies,* by Sirian Starseed Patricia Cori, and *El An Ra: The Healing of Orion* a novel by Solara, explore these Orion War ideas.)

**Alpha-Centaurians:** The Centaurs (half man and half horse) are beings who herald from the Alpha Centauri Star System. Alpha Centauri is the brightest star in the southern constellation of Centaurus. It is also a binary Star System and the closest Star System to our Solar System, and the Centaurs who herald from there were powerful warriors. Of course, anyone can be a powerful warrior should they choose, but Alpha-Centaurians do not fight merely to do battle and feed their blood-lust, they fight for a cause, or to uphold justice, or protect the weak.

During the Orion Wars the Centaurs were defeated, and the species destroyed. The Alpha-Centuarians experienced such total annihilation from the Draconian Reptilians that they carry their personal anger and rage in a very specific way. This was because when they were attacked on their home planet their DNA was disassembled, and the back half of the centaur (the horse), and the front half (the human), were separated by their enemies to weaken them and teach them a lesson. That is one of the reasons you don't say to a modern-day Centaur, "I'm going to teach you a lesson," unless you want to get kicked hard. And, they can kick hard! Early on in their human incarnations it is very likely that they fought anything and anyone that opposed them, or got in their way. As their soul matures they work for causes without a sword in their hand; but they can be just as fierce.

On Earth a Centaur can be either horse or human, and some have chosen to repeat incarnations as horses and others as human. Much of this can depend on which half they were on their home planet, but not always. If a Centurian wishes to avoid the difficult human karma, and remain in a horse body for many incarnations, they are certainly allowed to. Many of these horses are the ones who seem more intelligent and sensitive than the average horse. When they find their front half they bond intensely with their human, and when ridden by that human they will ride as one. In their heart all Centaurs are looking for their soul mate to complete them (the front or back half), and if the soul mate is still in a horse body they will love them like they would a human soul mate. Often, if they settle for a partner less than a soul-mate, they will be miserable.

Human-Centaurs have to fight desperately against an innate cynicism. They struggle to see the good in the world; they may desperately want to, but it can be a struggle. Their wounding is so deep that they often feel lost and abandoned, and can have difficultly meditating or connecting to God. The disconnection feels to them as if their very soul was torn apart, and it is difficult to recover from such destruction. Learning to "love your enemy as yourself," is the spiritual goal of anyone, but an Alpha Centaurian may struggle with this concept more than others. How do you love someone who ripped you, and your entire species, into tiny pieces and made it extinct?

Many of these souls will feel the plight of Earthly animals acutely, and work to protect endangered species. They might work in animal shelters or rescue strays. The Centaurs are *not* wizards. They do not do magical spells to destroy their enemies, as others might. They do not work in the shadows. They are upfront (what you see is what you get) types. They like their truth spoken plainly and clearly. If they lay a trap it will be in the 3D not in the metaphysical realm.

To heal their karmic wounding the Centaur-human must learn to stand alone, and resist the dependency they have on a soul mate or "other half" to heal their broken hearts. Learning to complete themselves with direct communication to the Divine will assist them to trust again; they will not feel so wary of others, or alone, because they feel the strength of their inner spirit guiding them.

They need action, not words, to heal. Working for a good cause or helping others will go a long way to making them feel connected to a family that holds similar beliefs. Coming to the aid of abused horses or other animals will assist them to feel they are doing some good in the world, and remove the helpless feeling that often plagues them.

**Lyra and the Fairies:** There are Starseeds who do not easily fit into other categories. This is because although they are ancient Lyrian souls, they fled the harshness of the Orion Wars and incarnated for long periods on Earth (and elsewhere) in what is known as the fairy realms. Here they hid out, hoping to find an environment similar to what they left behind. The Star System of Lyra gave birth to many of the creational templates, and it was where the cat template was first manifested. There are many, many advanced species throughout the Multiverse who are derived from the cat template, and they all worship their Christed Being: on Earth known as Aslan. Aslan was depicted as a Christ-Lion figure in the children's book, *The Lion, the Witch and the Wardrobe*. It is important to understand that the perfected "Christ-template" exists for each ensouled species.

Starseeds from Lyra came from a beautiful world of unicorns, rainbows and all the things that cynical humans love to poke fun at. Some of them had the bodies of fairies and could create magical sparkles with the wave of their hands. The evil that invaded, and soon completely claimed their home was too much to bear, and after searching for a home to land upon (like other Starseeds) they wound up in the closest thing to their old life they could find on Earth: the fairy realm. The Wee People, Leprechauns, Elves, Imps, and Fairies populate the fairy realm and hold open a fifth dimensional world both above ground and also inside the Earth in an inner world dubbed Agartha. The struggle for a human-fairy, and human-elf, is to hold truth without running away when they feel threatened by the third dimensional darkness. Coming into soul maturity for an ancient Lyrian is challenging; the longer spent in the fairy realm the more challenging the integration. Because they often choose to flee rather than fight, their inner warrior is sometimes underdeveloped. They will have to learn how to defend themselves, and reclaim their power by standing to fight, rather than fold, when appropriate.

Human-Lyrians, fairies and elves will naturally be drawn to all things of the nature realm such as aromatherapy, crystals, and herbs. They will also be involved with stabilizing and re-gridding the Earth to maintain balance in the face of dark forces who challenge their fifth dimensional realms. Because their systems can be delicate, they need to constantly monitor their physical bodies and make sure they do not put too much strain on them. Finding the balance between the dualistic Earth energies of good and evil can be very taxing on these humans, and it is important for their survival that they learn to take care of themselves emotionally and physically.

**Andromeda:** Like many other Starseeds, those who herald from Andromeda have a complex soul history. Much of it depends on the individual's story. Many Andromedans will resonate with sacred geometry and mathematical formulas, understanding almost intuitively how these building blocks are a part of the sacred nature of all creation. This knowledge was particularly useful to the Draconian army, and so when they enslaved the Andromeda planets to acquire the knowledge they did not destroy, they dominated. Human-Andromedans tend to fall into two categories: those who loath technology, due to their karmic role in the destruction it has caused throughout the galaxies, or those who are fascinated with technology because of their role.

It is important to state here how the Andromedan scientists were used by the Draconians to create a robot race, spaceships that could move through time and space, create cloaking and veiling devices, and the splicing of DNA between species. (It is not my, nor Merlin's, intention to repeat all the information contained in my previous book, *Merlin's War*, however, some of that information must be repeated here.) Many of these scientists are alive on the Earth today and their karma is quite evident in the scientific evolution of the Earth, both in positive and negative ways. Nikola Tesla and Albert Einstein, both of whom had tremendous knowledge of metaphysical and physical principles, have had their inventions and mathematical formulas used for both positive and negative outcomes.

As the Sirian Starseeds carry a great deal of Atlantean karma, so too do the Andromedans. The brilliance of the technologies used in Atlantis, such as harnessing the energy of the ley lines of the Earth (her acupuncture meridians) to power vehicles, are typical of the inventions of the Andromedan-humans. These inventions can be seen (both destructive and creative) in the modern world, as well. Scientific inventions are being used to both enslave and free mankind, and depending on how the inventions are applied, and into whose hands they fall, will determine which impact they have.

The Andromedan scientists have an important karmic role to play, but what gives them their brilliance, often blinds them to deeper awareness. The less brilliant among them won't believe in anything they can't touch, or at least prove with a formula, and refuse to open their minds to see what is often right in front of their faces. They are also deeply susceptible to arrogance, and when this occurs they can be insufferable. The Andromedans with this karmic imprint will benefit by humbling themselves to accept that they are not masters of all they survey, and that they have much to learn. Their resistance comes from the unwillingness to revisit painful past-life karma from a time when their inventions were the cause of suffering for so many.

On the other end of the spectrum are the whistleblowers. Those who attempt to heal their karma by exposing the misdeeds of others. Those who have worked in military, and other organizations that abuse power, and then decide to expose the injustice they discover there, are often working with Andromeda karma. Unfortunately, they often pay the ultimate price for standing up for their principles. They pay with their lives, or freedom.

*(I worked with an Andromedan-human who discovered that she punished herself for many lifetimes due to her karmic complex. While in Andromeda her inventions had been used to harm others: On Earth we might compare this to Einstein, a peaceful man whose brilliant concepts brought about the atomic bomb, which was used to kill hundreds of thousands. My client was abused and enslaved lifetime-after-lifetime due to the karmic complex she carried, which created a belief in her that she deserved to be punished. Through this I also came to understand how the Dark Forces will often target these individuals, making sure they don't reawaken their brilliant gifts, because otherwise, they could free people on Earth from the very devices they had helped to create.)*

Wealthy individuals, and governments, often control these individuals (because they have the money to support the research), and it is easy for their inventions to have dire consequences. It is important to note, for example, that many of the scientists involved in the development of the atomic bomb, or the space program, such as Wernher Von Braun, worked first for Nazi Germany before working for the US government. For many years after WWII, Von Braun worked with the U.S. Army in the development of ballistic missiles. As part of the military operation called "Project Paperclip," he and other Nazi scientists were brought to the United States. They worked on rockets for the U.S. Army, and became the precursors to the United States space program. The sides are always blurred for the Andromedan scientific mind.

The tendency, because they are so brilliant, is for them to believe that they are worldly and not naïve. But, in fact quite the opposite is often true; because so many of them can talk over the heads of average humans, the assumption is that they are smarter in all things. But, they are easily tricked because they do not always have fine-tuned sensibilities about human motivation and behavior—aka: street-smarts. Quite often they aren't interested in humans; they are interested in their work. They may think they know who is good and bad, but in truth their people skills in these areas are sorely lacking. Those of you familiar with the television show, *The Big Bang Theory*, will recognize *Sheldon Cooper* as a broadly-sketched Andromedan character. Growth occurs when the Andromedan-human scientist admits their limitations and puts heart and conscience before mind.

**Reptilians and Reptilian-humans:** All humans have a "reptilian brain." Also called the Triune Brain, it is said to be responsible for our more basic, and less evolved, impulses. Growing out of the reptilian aspect of the self is essential to evolution, and an argument could be made that the baser emotions ruling human behavior, such as jealousy and greed, are a direct result of the lower brain and reptilian functions. So, some might argue that all humans have some reptilian in them. The discussion of Draconian Reptilians, however, is tough stuff for most humans, so they will either discard it, run from it, poo-poo it, or be put into fear by it. It is rare to find someone who can listen to the notion that these beings exist, accept it, and feel enough in their mastery to actually bear witness to these ideas without a fear-based response. I suggest that you witness the events in the world around you and decide, without fear, what makes sense for you to integrate. Releasing fear is essential, this is not about doing a Reptilian witch-hunt. It is about self-mastery. We must clear our lower instincts, including fear, to be free from Reptilian manipulation.

Some believe that the reason we have this reptilian brain is a result of direct DNA tinkering by the Reptilian race when they first arrived on this planet long ago. Some believe that they genetically altered the human race by also unplugging our DNA from twelve to two strands. This was only one of the ways they have kept humans dumbed down and asleep. It is well known that the human race has been functioning with only a small percentage of their brain power being used.

David Icke, in his book *The Children of the Matrix: How an Interdimensional Race has controlled the World for Thousands of Years- and still does,* declares *his belief in* this area. According to this theory, there are humans who are more Reptilian than human. These beings, and their ability to shape-shift between human and "demon," is well-documented by many cultures and individuals worldwide.

*(I have witnessed a human being do this type of shape-shift right before my eyes; I was terrified, of course, at the time. But, I now understand what I witnessed. I believe I was given this event so that I could relay this information with the knowledge that it was, in fact, real. I also have*

*sympathy with those who have trouble believing this is true; I wouldn't believe it either, if I hadn't experienced it myself.)*

The Reptilian-human must curb the arrogance that often plagues them. They desire to be above humanity, and are often angry because they are trapped in the wheel of reincarnation. Being humble is quite a challenge to those with a great deal of Reptilian energy locked in their DNA and karmic memories. They can be quite brilliant, and tend to talk around or at most humans; but if you are alert you will notice that often the words they speak do not have a heart-attachment. They are smart, and slick but devoid of compassion or heart energy. To heal the self the Reptilian-human must learn to love the human aspects of who they are and the humanity in others. Awakening compassion and empathy are important if they are to join the dance of life. They must open their heart-center, and they can begin by feeling love and gratitude for others.

The Draconian Reptilians (from the Draconian Star System) are responsible for the origination of the Orion inter-galactic wars and their influence on Earth appears to be widespread. Although the influence of the Reptilian race has been evident for thousands of years, this information is just beginning to be understood by Earth humans. Most people continue to doubt it, for if they have not had direct experience with a Reptilian being, it is not a part of their reality. Fortunately, the combination of people waking up to past life and galactic memories, and people speaking up about their present life interactions with these beings without fear, is spreading knowledge of their existence.

If you can accept a lower ET, or inter-dimensional form of entity, then you might be able to accept that they are responsible for the lower matrix of control that rules much of the darkness on this planet. There are those who believe that this matrix of control originates off of this planet, elsewhere in our solar system. (Saturn and the moon.) It appears that the genetic tinkering did not end with the ancient human/Reptilian hybrids, but continues today through the work of human-Reptilian scientists.

Most people believe that a soul cannot be snatched. I believe that this is incorrect. At the time of death, or under intense torture to a point close to death, the soul abandons the body. The soul is an electromagnetic field of energy which can be captured and held. The Reptilian-based army learned, over many hundreds of thousands of years, and much experimentation, how to capture a soul and reprogram it. It can then be reinserted into the original body, or into a clone. Through implantation, much like a computer, the clone becomes under the control of the Handler. The soul has been reprogrammed. There are those whose souls appear dead, and unable to express human emotions such as compassion. Perhaps it is worth another look at why this may be true. Perhaps the soul has been compromised; or perhaps the soul is Reptilian of origin and not human.

Simultaneously, there are also humans who made contracts with the Draconians while undergoing intense torture. These individuals under duress of torture agreed to work with the Reptilians. If your journey to off-planet experiences brings up such a memory, then you were such an individual and may still carry the implant today. What is important to realize is that the contract to carry this device is under your free will to break; however, many of the individuals who carry this contact believe that they cannot break it, or do not desire to do so. It is very possible that the implantation and enslavement has been going on so long that it has become comfortable. The fear of breaking the contract is too intense.

Not all ET implants appear to be Reptilian in nature. It seems that many may be placed to track and study human beings. I have met a number of Pleiadian-humans, for example, who believe their implants are benign. Perhaps these were placed much in the same way we tag an animal, to track their movements and study their behavior. Are these implants being utilized to understand the human race better? Are those who agree to carry them assisting their ET friends to study and understand the human race? The implants which control human behavior and create violent reactions in their subjects are clearly of Reptilian or Reptilian-human origin. The implants which appear more benign may not control the owner of the implant, but track them instead, much as we track wild animals.

Whether you believe that the implant is detrimental, or not, it is my belief that the good guys don't need to put an implant into anyone, so any implant should be disarmed. To disarm an implant you will need to be free from the karma that attaches you to the beings that put it there. Declare yourself to be sovereign, and state your intention to disarm the implant. You will know where the implant is located usually by a bump, or irritation place. Many of the main implants are in the back of the head near the neck, and in the right or left temple. I have heard of implants everywhere, however, including behind the knees, in the ribcage, in the arms, or the back; any place can house them. Some people will have them removed in actual surgery, but often they can be energetically disarmed. Use light from the God-Source, and the sword of Michael to clear difficult implants. Those of you who resonate with the higher vibrational Arcturians will find them helpful in this assignment. You will know if the implant is disarmed because you will feel different mentally, physically, and emotionally.

It is important to realize that these implants don't create anything. This is not a "creative" force and because of that these implants can merely stimulate what already exists within the individual. If you have a tendency toward self-destruction, greed, envy, or sexual deviance the stimulation of the implant will heighten it; but it cannot create something that does not already reside within the individual psyche.

*(I recently energetically disarmed an implant in my client's right temple that had been put there by the Praying Mantis ETs, and my client's severe back pain immediately cleared up. I have also heard of a number of people having actual non-human, metallic implants removed by surgeons. I cannot recommend a surgeon for this, as I do not know one personally.)*

What about all the cloning that is going on today, and the talk of self-aware robots that we are creating? Is it true that if the being is soulless they engender no karma? It appears this is so. Karma is a soul-contract; no soul, no contract. Once the soul is reconnected to the Light-Source, karma is re-attached. Avoiding karma is a major intention of the Dark Forces, and they have learned a number of interesting ways to circumvent it. The creation of these robotic beings is one sure way; no soul, no conscious, no karma. Just like a computer is karma-free, so too is a robotic being. Also, the Transhuman/robotic movement closes down the heart-center and highlights perfected mental capabilities.

In some cases psychics have been implanted, and are under the control of Reptilian handlers, and they can be either aware, or unaware, that their power is not coming from the Light, but from the Dark. (Ted Owens, the PK MAN, claims to have been working with Space Intelligence in his abilities, for example.) Sometimes a psychic may have been in the contract for so long they can no longer recognize it. They do not know the difference between receiving information from the Dark Side or the Light. The simplest way to tell where the information is coming from is to ask, "Do I experience liberation from direct spiritual knowing?" A higher knowing is liberating and frees you, as it challenges you to look at yourself with clarity. If you feel challenged to grow and open your heart, you will know your knowledge is in alignment with your Highest Truth. It is not a voice in your head telling you what to think or do. The ego is the entry-way to the dark side of our nature and the Reptilian handlers cannot create something inside of you that doesn't already exist. In other words, they stimulate the wounded ego issues and prompt you to act from them rather than from your higher nature.

Being heart-centered in your approach to life is the clearest way to avoid the dark agenda. The Reptilian implanted self is ego-based, and knowledge is not used to liberate, and enlighten, but to enslave. Dark witches and warlocks are often implanted and although they appear to be all-powerful, and their clients marvel at how much information they have about the client's life, much of it is being downloaded from a Draconian source. It is our job to recognize an individual who is truly heart-centered from one who has all the right words, but isn't being honest. We can love everyone, but we don't have to give our power away to anyone! Loving another means you love them not only for their highest good, but for yours as well.

It appears from reports that Reptilians that have not been blended with human DNA can easily move between the third and fourth lower astral dimensions. They have been seen as ghostly visitors in the bedroom, or underground in caves. Both modern and ancient shamans talk of their encounters with these beings. They are fierce and powerful warriors.

*(There are those who report that the human-Reptilians can also move between the third and fourth dimension, and that they have created whole "worlds" in the fourth dimension; I have not had direct experience with this, but I suspect this too may indeed be true.)*

Most human-vampires have no memory of where they originally came from. It seems that they are a mixture of the Pleiadian-Dragon-Reptilian line. They were created at the time of capture of the Pleiades. They have a mixture of this DNA; they know they are different. Vampires have nests which are energetically fed by a Queen, much in the same manner that the Pleiadian Queen Bees fed their "children." Some of the Pleiadian Queens were turned by their captors to their dark shadow side and they became Vampire Queens against their will.

*(Recently I have been assisting just such an individual who is choosing to re-learn to feed from the Light and not the Dark. She is the most implanted human I have ever witnessed; plates were put in front of her heart chakra and on her crown chakra to make it impossible to receive Light. Many vampire parasites—her children—were attached to her and feeding off her; draining her. To free her is a monumental task due to the position she holds in the nest. Many of the energies were unwillingly to move to the Light and felt they were "starving" if my client went to the Light. These energies could not be forced to the Light; but the dark energies that remained understood that they would be required to accompany the original Queen host to the Light. Even with all the assistance my client is receiving from myself and three other healers the task of freeing herself is monumental. She gets an enormous amount of "kick-back" from the Dark Side every time she moves closer and closer to the Light. I am happy to report, however, that she is doing better with each session.)*

The myth of the vampire being immortal is directly tied to this desire to avoid one's karma. If you do not die, and you figure out a way to avoid karmic review, it is possible to live without payback. This has been a major goal for those who wish to do as they wish, and avoid the "as you sow, you reap" karmic contracts. It appears that the movement between the third and fourth dimensions, and body-hopping, is motivated by the desire to retain power and to avoid karmic review.

Vampires often present themselves as a beautiful, but poisonous "flower"; just like poisonous flowers they entice the victim to draw close with their sweet appearance, but trap them once the innocent victim has "landed upon their petals." Vampires are similar in their approach, using beauty and sweet words to lure in the innocent victims. To lure children, a Vampire Barbie doll is currently being manufactured. The sexy teenagers in the *Twilight* series are also seductive for exactly the same reason.

**EXERCISE SEVEN**: Reclaim your Starseed roots and heal the karmic imprint that you carried to the Earth when you began your Earthly incarnations. Neutralize the emotional reactions that keep you from your work. Humble yourself in service to humanity and recognize good and evil, up and down and as above, so below. The templates made in the heavens are all here on Earth. Learn to recognize the truly sweet, from those who seduce and ensnare.

If you suspect you have implants scan your body and ask your Higher Self to reveal any information about this. If you can disable these implants by working with your angelic guides, or the Arcturian healers, then do so immediately. If you suspect you will need to go to a healer, then ask your Higher Self to assist you to find someone that can remove or disarm the implants. Working with an energetic healer of your choice, with the intention to disarm the implants can be successful; the proof is in the pudding. Do you feel different during and after the session?

To gather galactic information it is very helpful to awaken fourteen chakras (seven of the physical chakras, located on the body, and seven off-body chakras). Meditate and begin to extend the chakra system out until you can hold all fourteen of the chakras in your energy field.

First balance the seven on-body chakras. With your mind, go to a place in nature that makes you feel safe and powerful. Next anchor the root chakra deep within the Earth. It can be at the mountains, or by the ocean, or a meadow. Then:

1. Place the 8th chakra about a foot and a half off the crown.
2. Place the 9th chakra into the sky and draw the energy back into your body.
3. Place the 10th chakra above the Earth until you can see the Earth below your feet.
4. Place the 11th chakra past the solar system until you can see the sun and all the planets.
5. Place the 12th chakra out past the Milky Way galaxy until you can see the Milky Way clearly.
6. Place the 13th chakra out into the Universe until you can see many different galaxies. Invite the angelic realm to meet you here. Notice the angels that surround you.
7. Place the 14th chakra into the Source, or Central Sun of God. You are now in alignment with God. Draw the energy down the chakra system and anchor it into your body.

Visit another planet. Explore what's there. Ask your angelic guides to show you a life you had on another planet. Each time you repeat this exercise visit another planet.

When you have become comfortable with extending the chakra system outward into other dimensions, or into space, you can also begin to make contact with the Arcturian Motherships that can be seen in our sky. On a dark, clear night go out and stare into the sky. These are *not* the clunky metal or cigar-shaped ships. The Motherships that are benevolent, and have positive energy, will appear as Lightships. In their multidimensional form they will often change color as you are watching them: blue, pink, yellow, orange, or green. The colors will dance before your eyes. Another way to connect to the ships is with Love.

The metallic cigar-shaped UFO or any ships that make your body react with fear or a loss of control are obviously to be avoided.

When you project out to the Arcturian ships with love in your heart they will respond by moving and dancing in the sky. Experiment with this and watch the light (perhaps you thought it was a star) suddenly move up and down and all around. When you cease the love vibration, the movement will also cease. Say Hello to your old friends!

*(I have done this with friends, and indeed the colored Lightships will move and dance for you when you send them love.)*

# Chapter Eight

## *Soul Contracts And How To Break (Or Honor) Them*

Soul contracts are contracts your soul makes, either between lifetimes while in the astral plane, or during your human lifetime, or any other lifetime (non-human ET existence included). These contracts can be good or bad and may exist for many lifetimes. Although it can be difficult to accept, we appear to make these soul agreements, or contracts, with other humans prior to incarnating. Our parents, lovers, teachers and friends have all come into our lives due to soul contracts, and so it is important to ask ourselves, "Why?" What karma are we trying to heal and break free from; or what karma is supportive and assisting us on our path?

These contracts are numerous. The contracts made in good faith, and with the intention of love, are not "soul-binding" in the same manner that a Family of Dark contract is. The Family of Light requires a pledge but the Family of Dark is less flexible in their agreements, as they do not honor free will. In any case, you have made an agreement at the level of your soul, and it is a much more serious and difficult-to-break contract than one you might make as a human; such as signing a lease, taking out a mortgage, or even marriage.

*(I never believed in dark soul contracts when I started this past life and spiritual work, but the numerous clients over the years who have told me of people they have known who have made them astonished me into a different point of view, and so I came to understand how real these are. When popular entertainers sing repeatedly about selling their soul to the devil, I listen to their words quite differently these days.)*

Karmic soul contracts with family members and friends are *vastly different* than contracts to work with the Dark Side, because everyone has karma. You cannot live without creating karma; it's how we learn. Make a mess, and clean it up, is a powerful teaching tool. When discussing a karmic contract we are talking about an energetic agreement. Karma is created when you take away another's free will, or do something that denies them their soul's truth or freedom. This can be as simple as a father denying his daughter the right to marry who she loves, cheating on a spouse, or as complicated as murder. At that time an energetic cord is created that binds the two (or more of you) together.

What does it mean to have a soul contract, and why is it so binding? If you ask an angel they will tell you that it is binding because you believe it is binding. Because you believe that it binds you, it will. The mind is very powerful, and it cannot be tricked. You cannot superficially think your way out of karma, you cannot merely wish yourself out of karma, and you cannot wish away a soul contract. Breaking a contract is a very powerful energetic move, and whether it is an agreement made prior to incarnating, or it is breaking an allegiance to the Family of Dark, it will be felt at the level of the soul. A profound uneasiness, and even fear, can arise when you first consider the idea of breaking such a contract. In some cases it was made because the individual didn't believe in the power of God to assist their cause; so why should they believe in God to assist them now that they are breaking the contract. In this case, the relationship to faith must change to break the contract.

## HONORING AND BREAKING KARMIC SOUL CONTRACTS

Karmic cords run between people who are emotionally tied to one another. These ties can be between a mother and child, lovers, even friends. These cords bind us, even when we are not near each other in the physical sense. They keep us close-by energetically.

Some cords you may want to leave in place; the cords that bind a loving mother to her child, or loving husband to wife are useful and wanted.

However, when you have taken the free will from another (or they have taken away your free will) a karmic cord is created that runs from your body to their body, and these are the cords that need to be broken in order for the karmic healing to occur. These cords will continue between individuals until they are broken. They will go from life-to-life unbroken until they are resolved.

The easiest way to explain how this works is that when you die your soul rises, and the denser energy will remain on the fourth dimension, lower astral plane that surrounds the Earth, while the lighter energy will move upward "toward the Light," as it is sometimes described. The third and fourth dimensions make up the lower astral plane, and the fourth dimension surrounds the Earth, and holds the energetic template for life on Earth. It is denser than the fifth and higher dimensions, and so it will be the repository for your "unfinished emotional business." When you reincarnate back on Earth your soul picks up the old energetic template, just like it is putting on an overcoat. It re-attaches to you, and depending on your soul age (and other factors) you will react to the karma in the new life.

In other words, you don't get away with anything. Karma is God's way of balancing energy; it is Universal Law and governs the lower dimensions. Emotion is "karmic glue." When you have karma you also have a profound emotional charge around the issue, and with the person. When you do a past life regression you will always find the karma is repeated again and again with a similar emotional charge, even if the actual event is not repeated. If you feel obsessed, terrified, repulsed, or angry you can be sure karma is lurking; even if you just met the person with whom you have the karma only five minutes ago. Good karma is sometimes called Dharma and that is associated with the talents and positive associations in your life. Currently we are not discussing this aspect of karma, but the bad karma that creates the difficult karmic bondage.

Karmic contracts can be made before incarnating; this means that they can be made while in your spiritual body between lives. Agreements to try and heal bad karma are made prior to incarnating, but sometimes when the soul returns to Earth the task of forgiving your perpetrator can prove to be too much, and the karma will remain to be dealt with the next lifetime. In more difficult cases the karma is added to, and the karmic soul mates will have even more energetic cords to break next time.

If you are attempting to break a karmic contract, and heal bad karma, the key will be forgiveness. Seekers who are in the Transcendental Soul School will have resolved all their karma, but those who are on Earth, and experiencing life as a human being, will be sure to have plenty of it to deal with. It is through karma that the soul learns its lessons. It is through their energetic cords that karmic soul mates find each other. The cords draw people together and make sure that they meet again. They ensure that the karmic soul-mates will remember one another— even if it is unconscious. Sexual attraction occurs even when people have bad karma. Sexual energy is so charged, and such a powerful force, it is common for people to mistake karma for true love because of the strong energetic force that karma brings to a relationship. If the karma has a sexual story connected to it, the sexual tension can be almost impossible to ignore; the duo will believe that they are meant to be together like storybook lovers, but in the end the emotional fire will be too much for them to handle, and what starts out as perfect can end up miserable.

All of these contracts are the meat and potatoes of life. They are very important, and not to be treated lightly. Murder, rape, theft, betrayal are all highly charged karmic contracts, and it takes a very Mature or Old Soul to forgive these profound experiences without using revenge to settle the contract. Revenge only increases the karma, and the emotional bondage will be carried over into the next life. A Mature or Old Soul will do whatever they can to even out the karma with peace and forgiveness, so that the contract can be broken at last. Baby and Young Souls are far more likely to seek revenge because they do not have the wisdom to understand what they are facing. It's important if you are a Seeker that you strive to understand your karma, and heal it with love not hate. Remember that what you do not heal you will face again in the next life.

People often ask: What if I can forgive, but the other person cannot? Does it take both people to forgive one another for the karma to be healed and break the contract? The answer, fortunately, is No. If you can truly forgive your enemy, and they cannot forgive you, then you can alter the contract by telling them (even in the astral plane through meditation and intention) that you are breaking the contract and that they must find someone else to play out the karmic game. If you have found completion and forgiveness with them you will know it because they will now feel neutral to you. They will not be able to trigger you to react in an emotional way again. When you can let them go; that's when the contract will be burned for you. If you are still emotionally attached to them the karma is still intact. Neutrality is the key to your healing. Freedom is the expression of that healing.

## BREAKING CONTRACTS WITH THE DARK SIDE

Now we get into the tough stuff because there are many people who cannot conceive of why anyone would be attracted to working with dark energy or people. Conversely, there are many people who believe that it is the only way to be safe in the world, or the only way they can ever have power. Using the energy of creation to get what you want quickly is one of the major seductions of working with dark power; it does not have patience, respect or faith that something good will arise from inaction. The Dark Forces take, and do not give back in equal measure, and it is for that reason they are called parasites or vampires. They do not think with compassion about the plight of other beings but always think, "What can they do for me?"

Many people will be tempted to skip this part, thinking that because they don't have a dark contract or any interest in the Dark Side in general, the information is of no use to them. But, as a Seeker you have the ability to consider things with greater neutrality. If, in fact, some people claim to have contracts with Dark Power, perhaps it is interesting to consider this a possibility and attempt to understand why this is so, and what these contracts are.

What if the battle between the Dark and Light is looked at as a battle between those who feed from the God-Source and those who feed from other sentient beings? Perhaps those working for the Dark Side hate those who work for the Light because they believe they will starve if too much Light pushes out the dark. It's a battle for nourishment: the Light needs the light and the Dark needs the dark. The idea of light and dark living side-by-side, with a dot of the dark in the light, and a dot of light in the dark, as expressed by the Yin/Yang symbol of Taoism, is not understood by those who believe the Light is superior, or the Dark is superior. The Taoists understood that both are necessary to achieve balance, but in respectful balance—as day and night, creation and destruction, respect one another. It is the attachment to Light or to Dark that creates imbalance, and the desire to destroy the other as bad.

The Seeker realizes that there is enough Light, and enough Dark, for both sides to live without starving, just as the day and night can coincide. The over abundance of darkness in the world is because the dark is greedy, and wants to eat beyond its fill, which causes the Light to push back, which causes the dark to push back, and endlessly the cycle repeats.

The human, who makes an agreement to feed the Dark Side, and bring it nutrition, is agreeing to create chaos, and weaken the Family of Light. It is their job to make more hell, and less heaven on Earth (of course heaven and hell depend on which side of the gun you are standing, as you remember that what is heaven to one side is hell to the other!) Those who sign contracts are promised wealth, fame and power to assist the Dark Side to gain nourishment, and they will not have compassion for those who stand in the way of their aims, because their allegiance is to those who need chaos to feed.

Sometimes, however, a person who has worked for the Dark Side for eons, and has found that the vampire nature of that side is weakening them, may want to change teams. Perhaps they have had an experience that leads them to believe they will be happier or better cared for by the Light than the Dark, and they want to defect. It is actually very much like the human spy vs. spy stories of traitors changing sides. The Dark Side will relentlessly attack their traitors to torture them, but the Light

Side sits by patiently, and watches when someone goes over to the dark, because they know that they must honor the free will of each and every soul. Much like a parent may do for a teenager gone astray, the Light will wait for the dark to exhaust itself, and come back home. This is because the Light believes that the dark's parasitic ways will ultimately destroy them.

When a human being experiences attacks from the Dark Side, paranoia often results. The Dark Side, especially through the implants mentioned earlier, will stir up the paranoia and attack the mental weakness of the target.

Usually, this is because the person does not understand the experience within the context of their reality. In tribal cultures the Elders would teach the younger members of the tribe about the existence of multi-dimensional reality, and prepare them to meet the world, both seen and unseen. In the modern world the idea of an unseen reality has been relegated to the insane, and so individuals are not prepared to meet beings on the other side of the curtain with knowledge and acceptance. What people don't understand, they fear. What they fear can make them paranoid. It helps to understand the methodology of the attacks to ward them off.

If humans were prepared to meet these unseen energies, they would handle an interaction with them without having an emotional meltdown. In many cases it can be a good angel, or a mean devil, it doesn't matter; fear of the unknown causes the human being to panic regardless of the entity's intention. If they were raised to accept and understand unseen forces, they might even become blasé about a dark energy: "Oh it's you again? I know what you are up to. I'm not interested. Go now!" Perhaps, like Buddha said to Mara, "I bear you witness!" the dark would flee when it is revealed. Every human must understand their right to be sovereign, and demand that these beings leave their surroundings when they mean them harm.

## PSYCHIC ATTACKS

If the Dark Side is trying to stop you, whether it's because they see you as a Lightbearer who threatens them, or you are changing teams from Family of Dark to Family of Light, you may have these experiences (and possibly more):

1. Voices in your head.
2. Energetic attacks that feel like being assaulted.
3. Intense ringing in the ears that will not stop. This is *not* Tinnitus! Do not mistake one for the other. (If constant tinnitus is your only experience it is biological, not psychic.)
4. The feeling of being followed and watched by vampires and other demonic beings.
5. Phone calls, emails and text messages from dark entities.
6. People turn on you: Friends or family members you thought were on your side, suddenly work against you. Are you paranoid? Is it real? This brings the paranoid insanity that can weaken you if you allow it.

*(These types of events are clearly documented in John A. Keel's, Mothman Prophecies, one of the most detailed books ever written about this type of paranormal activity. It records the experiences of many people. Some of these people include normal, small-town people from Point Pleasant, West Virginia.)*

These are a few of the methods the Dark Side uses, and they can be relentless. Some of my clients over the years have experienced all of these and more; those who most easily weather these attacks have a support system behind them that allows them to talk about what's happening without being labeled as psychotic. They are also able to feel love in their hearts even in the face of the attacks. If you know that love is a force of power, it goes a long way in the face of these episodes to assist you.

Nowadays, any event such as mentioned above, is deemed a brain imbalance, and the person is put on medication. I have found however, that the underlying cause of these experiences is not always chemical.

It is the job of energy healers, and Shamans, to look at the energetic and metaphysical causes behind such experiences. The most important thing for those who are being attacked to remember is that the Dark Side needs fear. It must put you in fear to destroy you. You can overcome that fear by knowing that Love will be stronger than fear.

Okay, sounds good, but here's the catch. What if you have been a Family of Dark member and you don't really know how to get in touch with Love or Light? Perhaps you have spent the last few thousand years believing in the power of the Dark Side and putting "down" the Family of Light because you believed they were weaker than you. It suddenly dawns on you that you have to make a whole new operating system, a new template, or paradigm, to operate from. You have to convince yourself that the power is in the Light, and not the Dark. That is very challenging for many people who don't work with the energy of Love or Light in an active way. This makes it very difficult for someone changing teams to feel safe, because they don't really know how to protect themselves through Light energy.

When a Family of Light member is attacked by the Family of Dark, once they understand the Family of Dark's operating system, and they have strengthened their power within the Light/Love paradigm, they are far more likely to withstand an attack without falling into paranoid behavior. They are able to raise their vibration high enough to resist the attack.

To break a soul contract with the Dark Side it is essential that the person breaking the contract spend a great deal of time making a connection to their God-Self and their Higher-Self, and to an energy of Light that they can call on: Jesus, Archangel Michael, Buddha, The Divine Feminine—the important part is that the energy you are calling on resonates deeply *in your heart*. Not your head. In your heart. It is through the heart-center that the soul is redeemed. Not easy for someone with a long history of attachment to dark power: but necessary. The Light Side will not punish you, but it does have requirements of entry (so to speak) and love and humility are two of the main requirements.

Next investigate why you are being held in an attachment to the Dark Side.

1. Did you believe at one time that it was the way to gain power? Did you agree to a contract?
2. Did you have karma to pay back?
3. Do you have intense guilt attached to the karma? Karmic guilt is toxic and invites dark energy.
4. Does your Light threaten them?
5. All of the above.

There are a myriad of reasons why you might be experiencing these events.

## PROTECTING YOURSELF

Fear is the entry key into your aura. When you are afraid your energy body is weak. Your physical body is weak. Everything weakens when you are in a state of fear. Fear is insidious and it hides. When most people are asked, "What are you afraid of?" they will answer, "Nothing." Or, "I don't know. Not much I guess." They are unaware of their fear until they are experiencing it.

Now put the same person who said, "Nothing," in a mine shaft alone, in complete darkness, and ask them what they are afraid of. They will think of plenty of things; the longer they are left alone the more things will frighten them. When asked, if they are honest, human beings will say that they live in a constant state of fear. Fear of death, disease, accident, heart-break, poverty, and abandonment . . . the list is almost endless.

When you were a child you knew what you were afraid of, and it hid under your bed, or in your closet. Becoming free of random fear and living fear appropriate is the largest challenge a human being has. The world has developed coping mechanisms to keep fear at bay. Even daredevils, who stare fear in the face every day, are acknowledging fear in their intense need to challenge it, and overcome it. Fear is part of survival and most human beings try to escape it as much as possible; however, in their need to escape it, they live smack dab in the middle of it, and they are constantly in a state of hyper-vigilance to make sure that nothing attacks them. The over-abundance of cortisol, in the bloodstream of most humans, attests to that.

**First:** The first and most important thing you can do to protect yourself from dark energy is to raise your vibration, by overcoming your fear of demons/devils. What you fear stays around, what you face dissipates. Love is a powerful weapon against the Dark Side. Love will enable you to see the divinity within the attacker, and weaken its attack. Use it as a tool to empower you, and bring the dark energy attacking you to its knees. You must develop a right relationship to Divine Energy, or Unconditional Love.

**Second:** You have the right to be a sovereign being, meaning that you have the right to declare what is in your energy field, and what isn't. Merlin's favorite saying is: "You shall not pass." This means the dark energy does not have the right to infect your energy field. Build a grid or barrier of protection around your body: this can include your totem animals, angels, Ascended Masters, or anything that strengthens your aura, and allows you to feel safely held within it. A mirror is very useful against energy sent by dark witches. "Whatever you have sent to me, I send, with love, back to thee." Imagine a reflective field that bounces the dark energy back to the sender.

**Third:** You have the right to declare what is allowed in your home, and what isn't. If you are allowing dark energy to infect your home, by inviting people into your home who use drugs and violence, then you have opened a portal to the Dark Side. You have the right to set boundaries and ask dark energy to leave. It does not make you a bad person because you do not want to be dragged down into the darkness. This includes friends and family members who are dragging you down, and bringing dark energy into your life. You have the right to say, "I will not go into the darkness with you." You have the right to ask them to leave your house.

**Fourth:** Make an oath to yourself to Love yourself, and value your life and your soul.

**Fifth:** Very important to understand this: Even a Shamanic healer or exorcist cannot rid you of dark energies if you do not do Steps One, Two, Three and Four. An exorcist of any type may release a trapped spirit into another dimension, but there are plenty more willing to take its place, if you do not do the personal work to raise your vibration another one will find you.

**EXERCISE EIGHT:** Did you clear out all your fears in Exercise Six? Exercise Eight is about looking at them again, from a different angle. Imagine that you are in the mine shaft all alone with nothing but you, and your mind, to keep you company. What arises for you that you might have overlooked previously?

Look at your history. When have you encountered dark/fear-based energy? What did you do to invite it in? What did you do to be rid of it? Remember when you have been the victim, and what you did to release yourself from it. Love is a powerful force, and every Seeker knows how to use it. Is there someone in your life that needs to be released?

Cutting energy cords: With your eyes closed visualize a person with whom you have negative energy. Where on your body does the cord that binds you insert? In your solar plexus? In your heart? In your throat? Notice and describe the thickness of the cord, and its texture. What are the ends of the cord like? Are they tentacles, or a sharp hook? When you are ready unhook the cord from your body, and present the cord to the person who inserted it, (or you inserted it into) say *three* times: "I release you. I release myself. I am free. You are free. We are free from one another with love and forgiveness, in God's name. Amen."

Fill the hole with love and light. Then select angels, guides and guardians to protect, and replace the cord, with a positive energy. Whatever you remove you must replace with something positive to fill the hole.

# Chapter Nine

## *Nephilim, Angels, Dragons And Reptilians*

*"And the great Dragon was cast out, that old serpent, called the Devil, and Satan, which deceiveth the whole world." (Rev. 12:9)*

*"The Nephilim were on the earth at that time (and also immediately afterward), when those divine beings were having sexual relations with those human women, who gave birth to children for them. These children became the heroes and legendary figures of ancient times." (Genesis 6:4)*

As I was writing this book (and *Merlin's War*) it became clear to me that there was an interesting, but quite complex tie between the Nephilim, Angels, Dragons, Vampires and Reptilians. So, before we go any further with this discussion, I want to clarify my point of view on the Family of Light and the Family of Dark. Are they an actual soul family? Yes, in a sense they are. When separation from the Source through individual identities first began, angels were created. These entities that humans call angels were the first beings created from the Source, and initially they lived harmoniously in higher dimensional realms of consciousness and vibration. Eventually, they began to develop personalities, and noticed their individuation. This separation led to angels experiencing the feeling of want and desire for the first time, which led eventually to what humans call "The Fall." Human mythology credits the fallen angels for bringing pain and suffering to God's world. Who are these fallen angels? Isn't it true, in some sense, that if we are here in this realm which contains suffering, that we too have fallen into density? Is there something to learn here? I believe in order to step from victim consciousness we must see the gift, blessings and lessons from our experiences.

As I was piecing these ideas together I knew that the first beings to fall into lower-dimensional density created the Dragon race. Dragons are densified angels, and they fall into categories: Red, Black, Rainbow (primarily green, purple, blue, pinkish and variations on that theme) and White. The Red and Black Dragons originally formed the Family of Dark, and the Rainbow and White Dragons formed the Family of Light. The Family of Dark is lead by a name that has become a cartoon: Vlad Dracula. The ultimate vampire. (Dracul means Dragon, and Dracula means Son of Dragon.) Satan goes by many names, and it does not matter what name you call him; but the angel Lucifer is not Satan. Archangel Michael was originally Michael-Lucifer, or Michael the Lightbearer (as that is what Lucifer means) and he sent the Lucifer part of himself into this 3D density. Lucifer is the Archangel Michael's shadow. Satan is quite brilliant in his rule over his Dark Family, and one of his smartest ideas was to turn the name Dracula into a joke, and to point the finger at Lucifer. With assistance from members of his team he has managed to make Dracula into a breakfast cereal, a perfume, a child's collectible doll and a sexy teenager; none of which lead you to the truth. There is a reason he is called, The Great Deceiver.

The Family of Light fell in behind Merlin, who befriended the White and Rainbow Dragons, offering them allegiance and protection when they were being attacked by the Red and Black Dragons. The Red Dragons have often been on both teams (Light and Dark) as they covet knowledge and power and will go where ever they need to go to get it.

The Family of Dark fell in behind Satan (Dracula) and so the battle was waged. The Family of Light fights to (among other things) maintain the human template, while the Family of Dark fights to (among other things) uphold the Reptilian template. *(To further understand, and make sense of this complex history, you may want to read my previous book, Merlin's War: The Battle between the Family of Light and Family of Dark.)*

What is important to know is that the Reptilian template, and the Reptilian family, have expanded under the Dark Dragon, Dracula's, rule, and they encompass many other created species: The Archons and the Demonics (mentioned earlier) work in conjunction with him as well. The Archons are robotic/demonic beings who guard the Lower Matrix. The Archon's God is a computer.

The galactic wars, known as the Orion Wars are, in many ways, an extension of the Great War in Heaven; the war between the fallen angels (Dragons), humanity, ETs, and the angels who remained in the Light. If the karma of every war on Earth reflects a galactic ET karma, and the fallen angels created the Orion wars, you can surmise that the Earth is still battling the ancient Dragon wars. "As above, so below." If you doubt if the angels of Light are involved in this war, then ask yourself, how many times have you called on Archangel Michael to rescue you from Dark Forces? By doing so you brought him into the war, didn't you? So, he is involved. If his shadow, Lucifer, is here, then he is definitely involved!

We are all familiar with the story of Lucifer's rebellion against God. We were told that Lucifer was jealous of God's attention toward man. (Here is the downfall of ego.) We were also told that when God favored man over angels, Lucifer rebelled, and decided to destroy God's creation. He tempted Eve with the apple, which stands for knowledge and lust, and awoke Adam and Eve to the existence of evil. His temptation and manipulation cruelly thrust Adam and Eve out of their Garden of Eden. If you were raised in a strict Christian religion this was told to you as doctrine; if you were raised in less strict surroundings, you believed it was metaphor. But where does the truth lie? Is there some truth in this? The awakening Starseeds, who remember being thrust out of their Eden-like existences on other planets by Reptilian, and other cruel beings, (as mentioned in the previous chapters), will see parallels to this biblical story.

The bible mentions Dragons, as in the above quote, and calls Satan a Dragon. Whose name means Dragon? Dracula's name means Dragon. Lucifer means Lightbringer. So, the assumption that Dracula is Satan, and Lucifer is Michael's shadow, is not so far-fetched after all. The idea that the Nephilim were created from a pairing of angels and humans makes more sense if we see it as a pairing of Reptilian/Dragon/Fallen Angels and humans. If Dracula mated with Eve, and created an angel/

human blend, and if Dracula is a Reptilian, then perhaps the idea of Reptilian-humans is also not so far-fetched.

The Dragon wings, and the color of the Dragon body, are an expression of the energy of the angel, and they manifest (as mentioned previously) in these colors: Red Dragons, Black Dragons, White Dragons, and Rainbow Dragons who are green, blue, purple, pink, yellow and variations on those hues.

Their weaknesses are generally this: Red Dragons suffer from arrogance. Black Dragons are bitter and morose. White Dragons are idealistic dreamers. Rainbow Dragons are naïve and childish.

Their strengths are generally this: Red Dragons are powerful warriors, and hold great knowledge. Black Dragons are mental wizards and can manipulate energy. White Dragons see the highest and best in others and empower others to awaken their inner knowledge. Rainbow Dragons are loyal and compassionate.

It is important to realize that not only are many members of the Family of Light deceived by this notion that Lucifer is Satan, but members of the Family of Dark are as well. The belief that they are serving Satan when they serve Lucifer is not accurate. The energies are different. Meditate on this a moment and you will come to the same conclusion—the energy of Lucifer feels decidedly different from the energy of Satan.

What is interesting to note is that the modern-day New Agers worship the Light, but so too do the members of the Church of Lucifer. The confusion is understandable. New Age websites might have references to the Radiant Rose and the Light. Then go to a Luciferian church website and you will see references to the Black Rose and the Light. The reason is because the New Age Lightbearers align with Archangel Michael, and the Luciferians align with his shadow which is Lucifer. But, in essence, it's two sides of the same coin. Much as you have an angelic or Higher Self who stays close to God, and a lower self who dwells in the third-dimensional Earth plane, so too does Archangel

Michael. Lucifer is the part of himself working directly in the third and fourth dimensions.

Archangel Lucifer can enter the darker realms, and still hold light, because Archangel Michael is such an enormous energy. Lucifer's positive side (yes, he has one) is that he can bring the Light, and illuminated knowledge, into very dark places. This energy is quite different from Satan; but few are aware of this. Lucifer's energy is not to be worked with directly, as it holds the great knowledge of darkness, but to be used in this way, "What have I learned from this challenging and painful experience?" Illuminate the dark with this question.

The name Satan is so highly charged, that it is difficult to wield it with any neutrality. The name Dracula has been reduced to fantasy and fiction, and this suits him quite well. Anyone today who speaks either of these names seriously is deemed a Christian evangelist, or a lunatic. This energy is the arrogant, power-hungry, pure evil that we know today on the Earth as the Devil. This energy will use all things to its own purposes without regard to allegiances. Many an innocent has thought it fun to be Goth because they were seduced by the teachings of the Church of Lucifer, and felt it to be empowering. But the Satanic energy is not illuminating, it is destructive. There is no loyalty among its members, and it operates *not* in the Light of Wisdom and Empowerment, but in destruction and greed. All its members are disposable; the small recruits will never be protected. They will never reap any long-term rewards by signing up.

When it is said that God and Lucifer battled over whose template would be supreme, perhaps it was really Merlin (Creator God) and Satan (Creator God). Perhaps they are both huge Creator Gods who are fighting, and God (the Source of all life) isn't fighting with anyone. Thus old stories of the gods battling with each other may be quite accurate. The gods can be interchanged with the Archangels and other beings from other traditions. They are named and renamed, but the energy is the same. The Greek God Apollo can be Archangel Michael, for example.

One can, therefore, conclude that both the Luciferians and the Archangel Michael Lightbearers are being quite well deceived by the being known as Satan, at least at the lower levels. The upper levels of the Family of Light and Family of Dark know the truth. Dracula has hidden behind Lucifer to protect his identity and keep people looking in the wrong place for the true evil. As the agenda of control and domination on the third dimension becomes more evident, it will also become more and more evident who is behind it.

The Galactic Family of Light (which contains the human template, among many others), does not align behind the lower Reptilian agenda, and fights to allow room for all beings to live in harmony. Whether it is with the Galactic Federation of Light, the Council of Ascended Masters, the Elders or Merlin's Seekers, these beings believe that the lower Reptilian agenda must be halted because it does not make room for others to share space. Those who wish to see balance restored understand that there will always be room for many beings to live side-by-side.

Is the information of the Nephilim (the children of the fallen angels) hidden to benefit those in power? Reports abound of strange skeletons found in North America and other places. In the 1880s, in a burial mound in Bradford County, Pennsylvania, it was said that horned skulls belonging to seven foot tall skeletons were found and dated to be around AD 1200. In 1924 skeletons of giants were found in Nevada. It is easy to find evidence of strange beings who roamed the Earth; but why is this information hidden from the majority of humans?

Although many people are waking up to the control systems, and trying to find an explanation for chemtrails, GMOs, and mind control programs, they still do not grasp the battle in its entirety. They don't understand why humans would poison other humans. They don't understand why humans are destroying animals at alarming rates. They don't understand why some humans want dolphins and whales, birds and fishes to die. They don't understand why "they" are spraying the skies with barium, aluminum and deadly chemicals which cause severe respiratory problems. Why are chemicals allowed into air, food and water that are clearly toxic to humanity? When chemicals are clearly known to cause illness, from lead to aspartame, why are they allowed in our paint that goes on our walls, and in the drinks we consume? Is it merely greed or is there another agenda behind it? Humans feel comfortable with the greed motive; it is one that we can all comprehend. But, is there another agenda hidden in the darkness? Perhaps those in control are seeking a different agenda than the majority of humans, but in order to maintain control of the human race they must keep the agenda covert.

The idea that there is a metaphysical tie to all this third-dimensional domination is beyond the scope of some people's grasp. But, oftentimes, those with ties to the angelic-Dragon-human template will feel it intuitively. The Starseeds will remember it in their DNA.

Humans are intrigued by the notion of royal bloodlines (the bluebloods), and why they are always in control of the planet earth, and bound together in their secrets and secret societies. What are they keeping so locked away? This idea has inspired many books and research projects. Are these beings descendents of angels? Do they have Reptilian blood? Is there a world, hidden from the average human that only the elite may join? Is our history different from what we have been told?

In the biblical *Book of Enoch* it states the original angelic names given to the angels who mated with humans are these: *Semjâzâ* is the leader of these fallen angels. The others include: Araqiel, Rameel, Kokabiel, Tamiel, Ramiel, Danel, Chazaqiel, Baraqiel, Bezaliel, Anaiel, Zagiel, Shamsiel, Satariel, Turiel, Yomiel, Sariel.

*And they became pregnant, and they bare great giants, whose height was three thousand ells: Who consumed all the acquisitions of men. And when men could no longer sustain them, the giants turned against them and devoured mankind. And they began to sin against birds, and beasts, and reptiles, and fish, and to devour one another's flesh, and drink the blood.*

This description could fit vampires and some of the dinosaurs as well. It is in that *Book of Enoch* that the term *Watchers* first appears.

*Watchers* refer to the actual fallen angels themselves, whereas Nephilim refers to their offspring. God gave Gabriel instructions concerning the Nephilim and the imprisonment of the fallen angels:

*"And to Gabriel said the Lord: 'Proceed against the biters and the reprobates, and against the children of fornication: and destroy the children of the Watchers from amongst men [and cause them to go forth]: send them one against the other that they may destroy each other in battle."*

To the modern community angels are sweet things; beings of light and goodness whose job it is to protect humans from calamity. And yet, in the *Book of Enoch*, God commands Raphael to imprison Azâzêl:

*The Lord said to Raphael: 'Bind Azâzêl hand and foot, and cast him into the darkness: and make an opening in the desert, which is in Dûdâêl (God's Cauldron), and cast him therein. And place upon him rough and jagged rocks, and cover him with darkness, and let him abide there forever, and cover his face that he may not see light. And on the day of the great judgment he shall be cast into the fire. And heal the earth which the angels have corrupted, and proclaim the healing of the earth, that they may heal the plague, and that all the children of men may not perish through all the secret things that the Watchers have disclosed and have taught their sons. And the whole earth has been corrupted through the works that were taught by Azâzêl: to him ascribe all sin."*

These descriptions are indeed far from the descriptions most of us grew up with. How do we reconcile the information of angels drinking blood with the halos and harps? The obvious choice can be to ignore the *Book of Enoch*; which was the choice of modern day religions. Another choice can be to consider it the wild imagination of the great-grandfather of Noah (who some believe Enoch to be). Others believe the Archangel Metatron was actually Enoch in human form. Archangel Metatron is said to the Keeper of the Akashic Library (or Library of God), and so he would certainly be the one to record such events.

In modern times the old stories are largely ignored. The angels are only loving and helpful, and in most cases humans believe that they don't ever take human bodies. Clearly, according to Enoch this is not the case. Who then are these descendants of the angelic line (why is Satan called a Dragon and serpent) and where do modern writers, who talk about the Reptilian bloodlines, fall in with this information? How far from our modern scientific perspective this information goes. We no longer are encouraged to look at this, and those who do are often considered insane for believing such a thing.

But, what about those on Earth who resonate with this information as truth? Those who not only remember, as was discussed in the previous chapter, their Arcturian lives, but also their lives in Dragon bodies? What about those who remember the ancient battles with giants and remember when these gods and goddesses ruled? Are these beings aliens? Are they imagination? Did the Nephilim just have misdiagnosed diseases? If so, then why do humans refuse to let go of the ancient tales? Why do they create and recreate them in video games, movies and television programs? Why won't they let this information go, or continue to resurrect it in modern-day versions of Reptilian bloodlines who rule the planet Earth even to this day? What if it's because some of the humans still hold genetic memories of those ancient times? What if the Dragons are not merely fairy tales?

What if the angels fell into the bodies of Dragons, spread out and inhabited planets, evolved in sophistication, and their story is an intricate part of All That Is? What if some of the fallen angels aligned behind Dracula and began a war on Merlin; not in fairy tales but in truth? What if the ancients remembered a history closer to truth rather than further from it? If you have remembered a life as a Dragon, always believed you could fly and know, without a shadow of a doubt, that you have great skills, it may be that you indeed carry the karma of the War in Heaven.

Those of you working directly with these bloodlines, in an agenda of domination, will more than likely not be interested in healing anything. You have the power of these bloodlines, and do believe in your superiority over humanity. This chapter addresses those who *want* to assist humanity to be free of this enslavement. Perhaps your karma draws you back all the way into the Great War in the Heavens. More than likely, if you are honest with yourself you will not have to ask; if it does, deep down inside you have always known it.

If you are here to help, whether you are a Titan, Nephilim or a Dragon, you will know that you are here to assist humanity to awaken from this trance they are living under, and to help them reclaim their right to live in freedom and peace. Perhaps you have been given the task of guarding great portals. Those of you who are guarding these portals—these Pandora's boxes—know too that you are being attacked by lower demonic or other energies to release your watch. Perhaps you are even guarding the Cauldron of the Watchers. Perhaps you are the guardian of the fallen angels who were cast into the portal. Where do you go for support? Where do you find someone who understands your task?

If the Lightbearers you reach out to have decided to support the agenda that says, "There are only love and light angels," you are even more alone. Now you are alone not only among the scientific community, and the majority of humans, you are also alone among those you thought were your peers.

It will take a very strong individual to stand up to all of those disbelievers alone. But, what if you aren't crazy? How do you deal with this karmic task? How do you heal this karmic imprint? Are you in a human body and given the task of a Titan? Perhaps you have betrayed your own kind (the Nephilim) and you are working for the Light, so now they attack you psychically? Who do you talk to about this? Who can help you, or shield you?

How do you tell if you are merely, as so many others would perceive, nuts, or truly holding such a large karmic imprint? If you are holding the karmic imprint in a real way, then every event of your life, from the time you were a child, and your first memories are remembered, will support this enormous task. If you are truly guarding such a portal, or doing such enormous karmic tasks, you will understand and know the ancient stories in your very cells. You didn't need to read about them in books, see them in video games, or reference others so that you would appear extra cool to your teenage Goth friends. You kept this hidden, close to your chest, and yet every event of your life quietly supports it. You are genuine and not derivative. You blend in with normal humans, and yet have understood how you are different since childhood. Not just special like mommy and daddy said; different in ways that sometimes you wish you weren't.

To complete this large karma, and heal the karmic tasks, the foremost thing you must do is to break free of the teachers you hoped would support your journey, but merely made you feel even worse. Your karma does not make you more or less special; it makes you who you are. Recognize this from a karmic perspective, not a special perspective. The tasks were given to you because you have an enormous karmic mission. Call it karma, call it dharma, call it fate, or call it destiny, it's yours, like it or not. You do not need to speak of it from rooftops. You do not need to proclaim that you are the only one who can_____ (fill in the blank, there are a myriad of them to choose from.) You do not need to proclaim that you are the descendent of: _____ to every Tom, Dick and Mary. Do your job, find those who won't run away from you when you reveal it, (a small handful, more than likely) and keep your mind clear enough so that you can hold the task and karma without falling into the seven deadly sins: lust, gluttony, greed, sloth, wrath, envy, and pride. These have taken down every human, Watcher, and Nephilim and everyone in-between since time began. Avoid them like the plague.

**EXERCISE NINE:** Ask yourself: Where have the seven deadly sins shown themselves in my life? Which one of these sins threatens to take me down?

# Chapter Ten

## *Sacred Tools And Symbols— Their Use And Misuse*

What are these sacred tools? In previous chapters we explored the desire for knowledge by both the Dark and the Light, and considered the possibility that the acquiring of knowledge is also the acquiring of power. It stands to reason then that both the Dark and Light have utilized these sacred tools for their own ends. Many Starseeds have memories of Atlantis or Egyptian lifetimes where using these tools led to battles between Dark and Light. They also have intuitive knowledge of these tools, and a desire to reawaken their knowledge and empower it once again, through a myriad of applications. Most Starseeds are also aware that a purification process is necessary to reclaim the use of these sacred tools, so as not to lead, once again, to conflict.

Sacred tools have been utilized by Starseeds to enhance their ability to travel multi-dimensionally, journey through space and time, open portals to other worlds, and awaken mental telepathy. The magic wand, Ankh, Holy Grail, Ark of the Covenant, crystal ball, Merkabah, and Excalibur are merely a few of the many tools that have been utilized by humanity. Each of these are powerful, however, it must be noted that in *theory* their power is essentially neutral and so any person or persons who wish to magnify their power can grab a hold of these and twist them to their own ends. Sorcerers with both good and bad intentions manipulate subtle energy to achieve their own ends. True Seekers leave their ego, lower-mind intentions behind, and allow a Higher Purpose to work through them.

Some of these tools, the most powerful of them, have been blocked energetically to keep the Dark Forces from accessing them and utilizing their power against others. Hitler's crusade to find the Holy Grail, the Ark of the Covenant and the Spear of Destiny is well known. He understood that whoever held these in his hands held the power to rule for good or evil, and he sent his army out to recover any relics they could find that would empower him. It is clear that the concept of utilizing magic is not only an ancient concept; indeed many realize that sacred tools are sought by modern-day humans as well.

Imitations are wide spread. Crystal skulls and ankhs are available for purchase in any New Age store. Most people who purchase these like to have them around because they remind them of a time when working with subtle energy was the norm, not an oddity. Modern-day dark witches and sorcerers can imbue these with black magic and create havoc for unsuspecting innocents. It appears glamorous to play with these tools, collect stones, cast spells and open portals, and most humans who do this have little idea what they are playing with. But, unlike the majority of these mass-produced replicas, the original tools contain energy that could possibly destroy a human who is not vibrating at very high frequencies. These energetic blocks protect the devices from misuse.

Some scientists have sought to recreate these sacred extra-terrestrial technologies with man-made replicas. The idea is to use a third-dimensional machine to replicate a sixth, seventh, or eighth dimensional sacred object. The earliest experiments to time travel are well known in the Philadelphia Experiment, and the Montauk projects. Their collaboration with the darker ETs in order to replicate their technology on Earth is also coming to light as they have sought to reverse engineer these devices.

What these scientists are proving to humanity is that the desire to live forever, and be invincible, has been alive ever since man became conscious; but the modern-day Earth technology on the third dimension has finally begun to catch-up. Many Seekers and Starseeds have memories of a past life when they utilized these devices for their own ends. Some of these memories are Earthly and others exist elsewhere.

The Egyptian Ankh has the capability to open portals to other dimensions. It is a lightening rod that can offer the wielder the opportunity to access other dimensional realities. It represents immortality because it opens up portals previously accessible only after death. If one can move through a portal and alter space/time then one holds the key to one's own immortality.

Did the Ankh ever have such power? Many people wear Ankh necklaces and have reproductions of this sacred object in their homes. What does it represent to them and why are they drawn to this sacred tool? Is there only one Ankh that has the ability to offer immortality or open portals to other realms or do the many replications have that type of power today? What does it stand for? Where did it come from and why? Like so many other icons on Earth it has remained a mystery to many people, or has become an empty symbol devoid of its original power.

The Ankh is essentially the ultimate spiritual carrier wave due not only to its shape (the human body), but also the imprinted intention. The subtle energy known by many as Chi, or Orgone energy, permeates the entire universe. Where it creates vortexes it also creates portals. It is no mistake that the Ankh replicates the human form of a head and arms and torso. The human body, and the Ankh, emit a similar vibrational quality. When the human chakra system is aligned and stimulated, including the off-body chakras, a vortex is created which opens a portal through which the initiator can travel. It connects the human body to the spiritual body which is timeless and formless, and allows the traveler to break the barriers of the third and fourth dimensions.

The Ankh is a transmitter and receiver of the Orgone energy; it intensifies the spiritual experience of space/time travel, assisting the individual who has aligned their chakras to move out of body. The Egyptians were replicating technology brought to the Earth by the star-people, and using it to reconnect to their Starseed homes. This technology freed them from the constraints of the third and fourth dimensions, and allowed them to travel freely. Although the human body was designed to be just such a carrier of this sacred energy without the need of external devices, because Earth's vibration had become so low, devices had to be created to free spiritual initiates from the web.

What a Seeker, or Starseed, understands intuitively is that freedom from the lower dimensions is a spiritual experience. The prison of third and fourth dimensional consciousness must be broken with a release from the lower matrix programming that keeps humanity enslaved, to allow the soul to break free and remember truth. A truth that has often made them appear crazy to others. Because this energy and knowledge is very powerful, it is essential that the spiritual initiate prepare themselves, step-by-step, to hold this energy before accessing it fully. As a result, the ancient mystery schools required the student to slowly increase their vibrational field so that they would not burn up or go insane. Select individuals were allowed entrance to these schools, and slowly instructed in the wisdom of these subtle energies. The mind, body and spirit had to be trained properly to access the secrets.

Modern man wants instant gratification; and so do many of the modern-day initiates. They are unwilling to accept the years and years of training that accompanies such an initiation. Maybe Jesus or Buddha had to spend half their lifetime preparing for their mission, but I want a week-long retreat to activate my Lightbody and a trip to the nearest store, or spa, to get my Ankh. Disappointment is sure to accompany such a request and emptiness of the heart signals the disappointment. Why haven't I found my joy? I was told I deserve joy and freedom! I am told that it is my right to get what I want. How come I haven't gotten it yet?

When ego accompanies such a request the person often looks to magic to fulfill the request. Their nearby New Age store offers classes in casting spells and moonlight initiations that gives the seeker hope that once again the mysteries will be revealed to them, and they will be able to manipulate the Orgone energy (the energy of pure God creation) to meet their own needs. They tell themselves, "I deserve to have my need met. I deserve to have John love me," and so justify the ego's fulfillment through witchcraft. The true Seeker knows differently.

Faith, trust and patience are the hallmarks of a true Seeker. When the vibration is right, the miracle occurs. A true Seeker will look to the Masters such as Buddha and Jesus to see how they had to purify the ego, and test their desires against the taunts of the Devil or Mara, in order to receive their full powers. Those who cast spells will eventually fall prey to their own spells—happiness will not result from the attempt to circumvent the true path. Spells are cast from the ego whereas true magic emanates from a much Higher Source of Power.

Hell realm is created by the misuse of these sacred tools; or the attempt to replicate them with third dimensional technology. Many a wizard has used the magnification of the power of a crystal to achieve their own aims but the Master understands the crystal is an ally to be used with love. A Master of the crystal knows that it is the crystal who is the true master, and the Master obeys the crystal, not the other way around. When Merlin chooses a crystal to place at the end of his staff he is well aware that it was the crystal that chose him. When Satan chooses a crystal he orders it to sit upon his staff and obey him.

The staff or rod is an instrument of sacred power, and it is for this reason that kings and wizards alike have been depicted with such a device in their hands. Psalm 23:4 reads: *"Even though I walk through the darkest valley, I will fear no evil, for you are with me, your rod and your staff, they comfort me."* It seems odd that the rod and the staff are mentioned in this passage as a tool of comfort. Certainly they are devices of support, objects we all lean on as we grow older, like a cane to help us walk. In this passage, the comfort is the cane of God, imbued with power to help the individual through even the darkest shadow world.

Throughout history this struggle has been recorded. It was said that the original rod of power was created by God on the Sixth Day, and given to Adam right before he fell out of the Garden of Eden. It was passed down through the generations until it was eventually stolen from Joseph by the Egyptian nobles, who planted it into the ground, and could not withdraw it, because they did not have the virtue (high enough vibration) to manipulate it. Only Moses was able to withdraw the rod. This story echoes the legend of Excalibur, and the Sword in the Stone. These sacred objects have been fought over since time began; those with high vibration are allowed access to them. Those without a high vibration: Keep Out!

As Seekers we consider this story of God and Adam and wonder if, in fact, the tale speaks of the Orion Wars. Did Merlin create a magical wand (or rod) and pass it along to humanity to empower mankind, only to have it snatched up by greedy and power-hungry Reptilian invaders? Is the Archangel Michael wielding Excalibur? Were these rulers unable to utilize the power of the magic wand because their vibration was too low to activate it? Have they been trying to get their hands on these powerful tools ever since? Did they create the atomic bomb as a substitute for the rod or staff of power? What other third-dimensional objects have been created by those who can't access their higher-dimensional counterparts?

Magic wands, staffs or scepters are related objects of power, designed to amplify the intention of the user. It is for this reason that both the crystals which imbue them, and the material from which they are created, are highly important aspects of the particular power they carry. Because each crystal carries a unique energy, and each material (ebony, ivory, oak etc . . .) has a different vibration, the combination of these (the crystal and the wood or bone) is a basic energetic element of the staff or wand.

Magic words are used to invoke a spell, and when used in combination with a wand or other power object they can strengthen the intention. Words act as a type of energy key that when used in combination with a sacred object, can open the portal, or unlock the ability to manifest one's will. A spell is, in essence, the lock of protection placed upon a sacred object such as a wand or staff—and it is the difference between something that is purchased at a store, and a true instrument of power. It is the difference between burning a candle and some herbs, and invoking a spirit. Of course, if you are interested in casting spells, there are thousands of books you can purchase that will tell you how to do this, however, this book is about empowering you to create the words yourself. In this way you know the energy is pure.

Abracadabra or "Abraq ad Habra" comes to us from Ancient Jewish mystics, and literally means "I create as I speak." Words, such as *Open Sesame*, which have come down through fairy tales and children's books, are examples of keys to the other realms. But, once again, many true words are protected secrets, that only the full initiate will be given the right to access. Only a true Seeker will be advanced enough to put their ear to the wand, and hear clearly the magic word held in the wand. Once again the word is revealed to the Seeker; the Seeker does not create the word. It is to be advised not to utilize spells that others have cast before you, to bring wealth, get a lover, or manipulate energy in any way to get what you want. The reason for this is simple; magic is not a trifle to be played with and many a witch-in-training has been overwhelmed by magic spells that they have cast. Only too late do they realize the power they have in their hands.

Can you be sure when you utter another's words that the words will truly serve you, and the Light and Love? The test is always with the heart and not the head. How does this feel in my heart? If you have doubts about the integrity of a given spell, or prayer, then honor your doubts. Perhaps later you will see it differently, but in the meantime listen to your intuition, and wait until clarity arises. You might be reacting from fear, not knowing; but pause until you are certain where the reaction is stemming from. Even an advanced soul can be tricked and have difficulty discerning a fear-based response from true knowing. Pause, be still. Do nothing. Get old fears, and old programs, out of the way. Follow the path of Love.

The Ark of the Covenant contains the magic tablets and the keys to creation. It also contains the original rod of power that Aaron, Joseph and later Moses had access to; meaning the secrets to using the energy of creation. (How do you think he parted the Red Seas?) It is not a "box," at least not in the third-dimensional meaning of that word. The Dark Side longs to possess it because it believes it will give them easy access to power. The truth is that these Ten Commandments, said to reside within the Ark, are the keys to using creational energy in alignment with Truth not ego. The Dark Side never realizes until too late that what they seek is the Light, and that to lift the lid on the Ark, and hold the rod of power before the initiate is ready, will unleash energy that the lower-vibrational soul cannot contain, and it will destroy them.

These instruments of power entered the lower realms with the assistance of Lucifer (Archangel Michael's other half), and many of the other fallen angels mentioned in the last chapter. These are the tools that God so feared mankind would misuse, and it angered him that the angels brought them into the lower realms. He was right, because power is a drug to the human ego until it has been prepared to hold it correctly. Returning these objects to their rightful place in the higher realms, to be accessed only by those who can handle their energy, is one of the essential keys to bringing heaven and Earth back into unity.

Ever since the daughter of Venus and Mars, Harmonia, was presented with a cursed necklace at her wedding, jewelry has been a favorite means for the Dark Side to attack the innocent. (Venus was married to Hephaistos when she had sex with Mars, and her husband was still angry over the betrayal and took it out on the product of their union, Harmonia. At Harmonia's wedding Hephaistos presented her with a cursed necklace, designed to curse her and her descendents.) The reason jewelry is useful in this manner is because it often contains gems and crystals that can be programmed to hold the consciousness of the holder. Many people who work with the Light will program these stones to hold positive energy; conversely, many of those who work with the Dark will use these stones to hold curses and dark intention. Although the stones can often be cleared with Reiki, sunlight and sage, many of these curses are far too powerful to be cleared in this manner, and if you have any doubts it is best to throw out the object even after you have cleared it to the best of your ability. Burying it in the ground should be done only if the stone has been cleared with Reiki first, as this is far more loving to Mother Earth.

Crystal skulls are another popular New Age tool for those who desire to acquire knowledge. It is said that they contain wisdom and the true skulls, like all crystals find the one they belong to. When enslaved they can be programmed and even accessed, but they will be unhappy and seek to resist the owner. The original thirteen skulls correspond to the thirteen original Ascended Master Life Creators, or Council of Elders, who are responsible for the creation of the Star Systems. Each skull holds their individual knowledge, and the thirteenth skull was originally held by Vlad Dracula (Satan), but when he fell and was exiled from his seat on the Council of Elders, it became the skull which held the accumulated knowledge of all the Elders; including Satan's.

The Council of Elders imbued the thirteenth skull with their collective knowledge so that those who accessed the skull would know the Truth of all Creation, and not merely Satan's point of view. The skulls are human in shape (not Reptilian) because they honor the human template.

It might be said that Jesus was given access to all twelve skulls through his access to the thirteenth. His initiation called "The Lost Years" prepared him for his task to hold knowledge held in these original skulls. It awoke the "God within Him," which is the keeper of all knowledge. It was at that time that he was prepared to undergo his mission to release humanity from the lower matrix, and remind them of their true gifts as Co-Creator Gods.

As a Starseed and Seeker you are on a similar, albeit personal, mission; one that cannot be shortened or made easy to satisfy the ego. You are a Seeker of knowledge, and as you begin to recognize that God is within you, you also begin to realize that, so too, is all knowledge.

The right use of will: It is in many ways the theme of this chapter. A Seeker or Starseed can be tempted to use their will incorrectly, and to awaken their power without taming the ego. When this is done the sacred symbol becomes a deadly symbol. Dark energy will utilize the lower device or symbol as a portal because the vibration of the user is not high enough to ward off such an attack. Ouija boards, pendulums, and tarot cards are all neutral devices which can be utilized by either dark or light intentioned energy; the Dark's intention is to manipulate the user, the light's intention is to inform and enlighten.

There is another type of individual who is actually quite common: fence-straddlers. These individuals want power and will go to whichever team they believe will give them access to it most quickly. They get want they want from either side, and believe they are more powerful than either side. They believe they have out-witted both the Dark-Lighters and the White-Lighters, and that they can use the techniques and wisdom of both sides without being trapped by either. They also have disdain for both sides (although they will appear to be aligned with whatever side they are hanging out with at the time), and have an aura of arrogance about them. They are the double-agents of the magic world.

These individuals form relationships that don't last long. They get what they need from the individual they have attached to, and when that proves troublesome for any reason, they attach to the next person they believe will empower them. They are always looking for the most power. Spiritual concepts such as unconditional love prove too challenging for them, because it requires that they move into an expression of power that they perceive as weak. The need to feel powerful and erase vulnerability is what haunts them and draws them to the darker expressions of magic and personal creation. Forever seeking outside themselves they have forgotten that the power lies truly within the purified soul. Reunion with Mother/Father God's pure creational energy cannot be manipulated. Merlin's Seeker school is tough training ground, and no steps can be avoided.

## SACRED SYMBOLS

Many tomes have been written about sacred symbols and if you are a Seeker or Starseed who meditates and heals, or a practitioner of Reiki, or even of Wicca, you already use many of these in your practices. Like sacred tools, sacred symbols are utilized for their power. Many of them can be found throughout time and cultures, and they are repeated over and over with no clear understanding of how or why they seem to pop up everywhere. Like sacred tools they can be utilized for good or evil, depending on intention. Many people realize that the Nazi party's Swastika is an ancient symbol found in many cultures, and it has appeared on every continent. It is found on Greek pottery,

Norse weapons, and Buddhist scriptures and in Native America rituals. It symbolized positive greetings and energy. Yet, most of us in the modern world know it as a symbol of evil and control, as it was expressed by the Nazi party. This is the perfect example of how a symbol can be corrupted and used by dark energy. In this case the symbol was inverted and imprinted with dark intention. Each time someone stares at it, an exchange of energy is completed; the symbol imbues the viewer, and the viewer imbues the symbol. The Pentagram, a five-pointed star with positive symbolism, suddenly becomes a symbol of evil when inverted, and used by the Satanists. Why do these have so much power? In part it is because human consciousness imprints these symbols with energy, and then the symbol reflects the energy of the imprinted consciousness back at the viewer.

The spiral is another symbol which is universal. It represents vortex energy; where a vortex exists, a portal opens. Once again, portals can be opened to access positive healing energy; but they can also be opened to allow demonic energy entry into the third dimension. The spiral is neutral, the energy accessed through the portal is determined by the intention of the one who uses the spiral, and opens the vortex.

Healers use the spiral to intensify the healing energy of God and this is why it is depicted on the healer's hand below. The spiral symbolizes the energy portal that opens when a healer channels healing energy to the patient. The spiral also symbolizes life creation and the womb, because it is through a portal that the energy of life enters the womb. The spiral is as ancient as mankind itself, and can be found throughout the world carved into stone and painted onto walls.

The spiral moving up and away, takes energy out. The spiral moving down and toward brings energy in. The chakras spin and spiral and all of these are indications of the portal that is opened with the vortex/spiral energy. Reiki practitioners use the Cho Ku Rei spiral energy to bring energy in to the patient, and also when reversed to take energy out. It is also used for protection, because when you bring in positive energy, it protects you.

The Flower of Life appears on the Temple of Osiris in Egypt. It is an ancient symbol that has spiritual meaning to many different traditions.

Leonardo DaVinci's Flower of Life also expresses the energy of this sacred symbol; it represents the building blocks of life, and Seekers use this energy to create life. Here it is depicted in two dimensions, but like the Merkabah, it comes to life when seen in a multi-dimensional form. The sacred geometry depicted in the Flower of Life represents the complex interweaving of dimensional reality, and how it combines to create existence. Human life is far more complex than we can fathom; each of us is tied together by energetic cords that reach throughout time and space. When we act in the present moment, we impact every other moment that has or ever will be. Well beyond our ability to conceive, the Flower of Life reminds us of how we are all connected, and interwoven in this multi-dimensional universe. At a hyper-dimensional level it is the expression of the manifestation of life.

On the other end of the spectrum, but every bit as powerful is the simple symbol for God, or the Central Sun.

If you think simple means not powerful try drawing it over your heart or head chakra and feel the energy. It is anything but weak.

The Caduceus has undergone many transformations. The depiction that is typically made today is of a winged staff with two coiling snakes. The original symbol of one snake around one pole has been replaced with a friendlier version of the healing energy even though it actually depicts the staff of Hermes (or Mercury) the Messenger God. The coiling snakes can now be said to represent the Kundalini Earth energy as it winds around the central channel of the spine, and the wings represent the spiritual or heavenly energy as it depicts the blending of spiritual and Earth energies in proper alignment for healing. This is a far cry from the Rod of Asclepius (the Greek God of Healing and Medicine.) This is the original depiction of the staff used by Asclepius the God of Healing.

One of the most important symbols is the intersection of pyramids or the intersection of V's. When completely intersected they represent the Merkabah. Although it might surprise some New Age enthusiasts, the Merkabah is a school of early Jewish mysticism, and the idea of the Merkabah is a chariot you can ride to the heavenly throne of God.

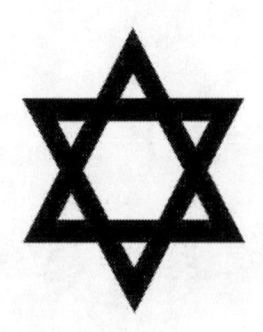

This is the Star of David, a two-dimensional depiction of the Merkabah. What is most important to notice about the image is the two pyramids combine to move the energy toward heaven and Earth. This bridges the energy between the spiritual and heavenly realms, and so carries the soul back and forth between both realms. When depicted in a multi-dimensional manner, such as in the Merkabah, it carries the soul between dimensions. Like the sacred tools, one must be prepared for the journey by raising the frequency of not only the mental and emotional bodies, but the physical body as well.

This is the greatest difficulty presented by using all of these tools and symbols: raising the energy of the physical body, not just the spiritual body. Combining the energy of the spiritual and physical body, and performing miracles with the physical body, requires the need to purify not only the emotional, mental and spiritual bodies, but also the physical body must release fear.

**EXERCISE TEN:** Place three different symbols in your third eye and hold them there as long as you can. First, hold the circle with the dot inside, which depicts the Sun or God. Feel the energy and decide for yourself how it feels. Next, place the spiral in your third eye and hold it there. Feel the energy and decide for yourself how it feels different from the first energy.

Choose any other symbol of your own and experiment with placing it in your third eye and feel what happens.

Next: Allow a sacred tool to reveal itself to you. It can be a crystal, wand, ankh or anything of your choosing. Listen to its message. Honor its lineage. Humble the ego.

Become a Seeker through the right use of will, and notice in your own life where the wrong use of will has wanted to assert itself. Have you ever been tempted to use the sacred tool or symbol for personal gain? Vow to use the energy for the Highest Good of All Concerned.

Create a staff of power for yourself in any dimension you wish. Hold it in your hand and feel what response you have to it. Allow it to empower you.

# Chapter Eleven

## *Death And Dying*

Dying and death are the greatest mysteries that human beings encounter. From a Seeker's point of view the idea that death is not the enemy is absolutely essential to freedom. Understanding that death can be viewed not always as tragedy, but at times as a gift, is important to feeling comfortable with accepting its presence in the world. Every religion has created complex rituals around the experience of death, and these rituals appear to be evident even in the most ancient civilizations.

Is death necessary? Is death real? Does death mean the end? A beginning? Release? Hell? Heaven? Most people's heads spin with these questions, and in order to feel more comfortable with being alive, answers have been created to put people at ease with death. But, what do people actually know of death? Because of modern medicine, more and more people are having near-death, or even total-death experiences, and coming back to life with stories of what greeted them. They have "proof of heaven," or in some cases hell. Atheists will argue that it's all a chemical reaction in the brain, and yet there are cases where the chemical reactions have stopped, but the human swears they experienced an after-life.

*(Proof of Heaven, by the neurosurgeon, Eban Alexander, M.D., tells of his near-death experience. His expertise gives him the added ability to speak professionally about how all of his brain functions had stopped—for far too long for it to be mere chemical reactions—before he was resurrected.)*

When the body dies, what is left? Consciousness? Emotion? The soul? Anything? Millions of people have been contacted by dead loved ones. Mediums have television shows to prove that the veil between life and death is thin. People quote the idea that energy cannot die, but merely changes form, as scientific proof of after-life. But, in the end the only thing that really matters is what you believe. Why? Because in the end when your physical body dies, all that's left is the energy body, and the consciousness that is attached to it. You indeed create your reality.

*(One of the oddest and most interesting experiences I have had of being contacted by a dead person, who asked me to deliver a message, happened with the miscarried brother of a client of mine. She had never known him, because he had never been born. She is now middle-aged, and yet his soul came to me and told me to deliver the message that he loved her, so that he could pass on. To prove it was real he kept saying, "Bosco. Not Ovaltine, Bosco." I remembered these chocolate drinks from my childhood, but wondered why he was saying this. I finally agreed to deliver the message because he wouldn't leave me alone. When I told the woman, "Bosco, not Ovaltine," she was astonished. She told me, "We loved Bosco and hated Ovaltine, when I was a child." It showed both of us that the miscarried soul was hanging out at the kitchen table while the children drank their favorite chocolate drink!)*

I have noticed through all the years I have been leading past life regressions, and taking people through the death experience, that each soul age experiences death differently. Each culture experiences death differently. Each person experiences death differently, and every one of your deaths throughout time and space will be different. Once the body is shed, consciousness is free, and creation is unencumbered by physical density. As a result, the individual's thoughts are of prime importance to the experience.

The more a person's consciousness is focused Earthward at death the denser the energy, and the more likely that a ghost will be hanging around to finish its business. The more a person is ready to leave, the more likely they are to ascend. I have also noticed that the younger the soul age the more likely the soul will not know "where to go." The older the soul age the more likely that the soul lifts quickly to a heaven realm and remembers how to maneuver the death experience.

Contrary to popular belief ghosts are not always miserable, and in fact they can be quite happy and content to hang around for awhile. They are doing just fine, thank you. They might be trying to reach out to a loved one, and have a message that needs to be delivered before they move onward and upward. They might be concerned about someone they left behind, and feel they need to be close to them to provide comfort.

There are a myriad of reasons that someone's energy might hang around after they have died and it is wrong to assume that the ghost is unhappy. The loved one might be suffering from the loss, but the ghost can be in a happy and peaceful place. However, it is best for the dead loved one to move on and not to linger; then they can return and say hello now and again to their friends still alive on Earth. When you smell the cologne, the pipe tobacco, or perfume it is a sign that your loved one is with you. They also might take form as a bird, butterfly, or other animal in nature. The message is often "Hello, I'm doing fine."

Once the message has been delivered, the loved one comforted, or the issue resolved the ghost will often move on of their own accord. Sometimes guides and angels, this is where the tradition takes over, will come and comfort or lead the soul to heaven. Dead family members can be met and reunion with one's soul group can take place.

Death is an extremely creative process. There are times when a soul will be afraid to move on; they will fear the Light, and fear to trust a spiritual presence other than their own, and find that they don't want to move their consciousness away from the Earth. This is when loved ones on the Earth-side of the veil can be very helpful to the dead loved one by reaching out to them through prayer and meditation, talking to them, or visualizing them and assisting them to move on and ascend upward. It is not necessary to perform rituals to do this, although those can be effective, if both the sender and receiver relate to the ritual. What can also be helpful is for the loved one, still on Earth, to send comforting energy to the dead loved one; picture a helpful spiritual energy reaching out to the dead loved one, and providing reassurance. In time the ghost will feel comforted, and eventually they will agree to check out a new location. If a message from your dead loved one must be delivered, agree to hear the message. Talk and dialogue with the dead loved one, and reassure them that they can move on. Tell them you'll be fine without them.

As I mentioned previously, each soul age also experiences death very differently. Unless they have been taught where they will go after death, Infant and Baby Souls are far more likely to get confused when they die. They often hang around their bodies, and watch and wait to figure out what's next. Sometimes they go quickly into another body; other times they eventually grow tired of watching the Earthlings, and decide to move on and "float away." Rituals are extremely helpful to assist in passage for these younger souls, and just like in life where they felt more comfortable with strong boundaries, so too do they enjoy the boundaries provided by strict rituals. They will see Jesus or go to whatever spirit they have been told will greet them in whatever manner they have been instructed.

Old souls are more likely to go immediately into the Light, and experience unity consciousness, and a feeling of immediate liberation. It is far rarer for an Old Soul to stick around, and they often welcome the freedom that death provides the soul. Again, death is a creative experience, and just as in life there is no one way to live, it is also true that there is no one way to die.

But what about the people who do evil? The people who are practicing Satanists? The ones who reject the Light? Where do they go? Does the Light force them to accept its presence after death? Once again it is a creative process. Sometimes a soul who feels great guilt will create a type of hell for the self. Releasing someone from hell can be difficult if they don't want to be released. Lost Souls are human souls who feel trapped. If their consciousness breaks through the curtain to impact live humans they can be difficult to reach because they don't want to move out of the world they are creating. Just saying to a Lost Soul, "Go to the Light," is not going to move them upward, and in fact you can experience energetic retaliation from the suggestion, such as things flying off the walls. They can be in fear of moving on for many reasons. Knowing what you can impact and rescue, and what you can't, is important because you don't want to tackle anything above your ability to handle it.

Every person thinks they can handle it until they meet the energy that they can't handle. Free will still exists for the ghost, and their free will doesn't allow a human to remove them. A ghost is still a human spirit and their free will is still in control; that is why Lost Souls and poltergeist are so hard to remove. You have to establish a bond and you cannot force them over.

Here are suggestions for reaching and crossing a Lost Soul:

A Lost Soul can be afraid to cross because they are concerned that God will judge them harshly. In this case it is important to explain to the soul that God is a loving and forgiving God, and that whatever they are concerned about was necessary in their soul's evolution, and will be forgiven if they are willing to ask for forgiveness.

You can let the soul know that God doesn't care what you were; He only cares who you are right now! Your mistake was not a mistake in God's eyes and he loves and forgives you. Explain to the Lost Soul that they are the toughest critic of themselves, and it is not God that causes the torment, but they cause torment to themselves with their own fear.

God is peace and love and does not torment anyone. Your torment can be over at any time; it is your own free will doing this to you. Peace and love are waiting for you.

Let the Lost Soul know that heaven can be anything they wish it to be. If the soul is uncomfortable with angels explain to them that they can be reunited with anyone they wish. They can create their own heaven. (I told a ghost once that he could have NASCAR, pizza and beer. He said, "You're kidding?!" I said, No, it's your heaven after all," and he moved. If I had told that soul to go to the angels it wouldn't have worked to move him.)

If the person was an animal lover then remind them that they can see a beloved pet. Tell them to look inside your heart and see, and know, that these words are true. Tell them "Release yourself from your own punishment and be once again in the Light. Forgiveness is yours."

Many religions teach that people who commit suicide or other sins will go to hell, and if the person believed it in life, then they may believe it in death. As a result, the person will create a kind of hell for themselves on the other side of the veil, and not ascend. Because you create your own reality after death, some souls will get lost and believe they deserve to suffer. If the Lost Soul is a loved one then it will be easier to reach them, and give them the love and forgiveness they crave; if you have just walked into a house that has a Lost-Soul poltergeist already haunting it, it can be more difficult to move the energy. However, the thing to remember is that the difference between a Lost Soul and a demon is the fact that a Lost Soul has a human soul; a demon does not.

Because of that, this will not work on demonic energy, and it is important to understand that demonic energy is not human. It does not have the same issues, or the same free will that a Lost Soul has. In fact it is not ensouled in the same manner, and as explained earlier, it is parasitic in nature. It feeds off its human hosts. A demonic energy is far more likely to mock God, and will not respond positively to the idea of going to God, or the Light.

*(My first encounter with this was twenty years ago, in my work as a past life therapist. When the demonic energy exploded out of my client: it cut my phone lines, threw things around the house and said, "You don't know who God is!" in a voice that sounded like pure evil, and then threatened me very strongly. This was at my suggestion to "Go to God, and the Light." I like to say the angels threw me into the deep end of the pool, as this was quite early on in my career with this type of work. However, it taught me and the angels did rescue me that night with their strong, comforting presence.)*

How about death and karma? The most important thing to understand is that karma does not follow you into the upper realms; but it *does* stick around in the fourth dimension, and wait to be picked up at a later time. The easiest way to imagine it is that karmic energy is heavy, unresolved energy that cannot ascend to a higher dimension of pure love and light.

It bears repeating that humans are responsible for their karmic creations and will pick up the unresolved karma upon re-entry to the Earth. Karma with the same individuals often repeats again and again until it is resolved, and past life therapy will show you that the same individuals appear again and again throughout many lifetimes. Some lesser karma can be worked on and resolved in-between lives, but the most difficult karma must be addressed on the third dimension, and cannot be resolved in the upper dimensions after death. Although it is possible to meet your enemies and try to resolve karmic conflicts with them while in the astral plane, there is no guarantee that the individuals will respond positively merely because you are now in another dimension. Many of you who have done past life regression have experienced meeting an enemy in another dimension and have found that forgiveness is not being given by them. The soul is still holding onto the karmic issue, and won't let it go. In this case it may be necessary to meet the individual on the Earth plane once again, and resolve the issue in the next life.

Again, the issue of karma and forgiveness is ruled by free will; each individual is responsible for their creations on both sides of the veil, and in all dimensions. The exception to this is the Bodhisattva or Transcendental Soul who is a soul who has burned all personal karma but chooses to come back to Earth to clear karma that they themselves have not created; they have a mission and a willingness to take on another person's karma and assist them to clear it. These souls will often take very stuck and difficult-to-clear karma; something which has been around for a long time, and the original owner of the karma has been unable to resolve. The Transcendental Soul is able to transmute difficult issues, and move stuck energy that a younger, less-experienced soul finds impossible to heal. This is often done by "walk-ins" or souls who enter a body not through birth but by "walking-in" to a body, and doing a soul exchange. The original soul moves into the higher dimension, and the new soul takes its place, and often agrees to clear the karma of the body it has entered. This is not a possession; it is done by loving agreement.

It is important for a Seeker to become comfortable with death as a transition of energy from one state to another, and to realize that attachment to their human identity is like attaching to anything on the third dimension: it is dust in the wind. Although the body, and life, is precious it is not the end all and be all, but just one journey of the soul throughout time and space. It is important to realize that loved ones, and family members, are also just traveling through time and space, and that someone may be your child in the current lifetime, but in the last lifetime they were an aunt, uncle, or friend. Every soul is on their own path, and although every soul is connected to every other soul through the One or God's Body, every soul is on its own personal, creative journey, and it cannot be dictated by another.

Having few regrets, and only minor karma, makes the transition from life to death easier. So too, does preparing for the experience by overcoming fear, and not overly attaching to the third dimension prior to facing ones' actual death. Instead of running from death, and denying its existence, embrace the notion that all things live and die, and that evolution depends on change and growth. Stagnation is not death. Stagnation is the same old mistakes, and patterns, repeated over and over, and that is truly hell. Acceptance that death brings release, not pain, is essential to a smooth transition. There is something on the other side: you! Because everywhere you go, there you are, making peace with yourself and those around you will allow you to let go without fear and regret.

**EXERCISE ELEVEN:** Contact a dead loved one, and have a conversation with them either by channeled writing, in a journal, or in your mind. Allow the loved one to tell you what they are experiencing, and how they are doing. Realize that you never "lost them," but they merely changed form!

# Chapter Twelve

## *Knowledge, Truth And Freedom*

It is now understood that Seekers are knowledge-gatherers and keepers. It is also becoming clear to any of you who have gotten this far in the book that both the Dark and the Light long for it. How they gather it, and what they choose to do with it, is what differentiates them. The eternal quest to seek truth is a challenging endeavor on a planet coated in falsehood.

There are many studies which show how reflexive our lying is. In one study the individuals were asked to talk for ten minutes. When the tape was analyzed the subjects told an average of 2.92 lies, without their realizing it. Other studies show that we lie at least four times a day. Even at that rate we are lying 1460 times a year. The average person has told about 88,000 lies by the age of sixty. It does not state in these statistics that the individual is a bad person and that only bad people lie. It takes all people into consideration. Of course, a lie is only a lie when it is said to be counter to the perceived truth of the individual. In other words, a lie is a lie only when you believe you are telling it. If you lived in the fourteenth century and you stated that the world was flat, and that traveling too far would lead to your falling off the edge, you would not be engaged in a lie. You would be engaged in belief-telling. You would be passing on your beliefs as truth even when, in fact, they were not. Once humans traveled great distances and never fell off the Earth, or flew in airplanes, and saw the Earth from a different perspective, they spoke their truth about this subject matter quite differently. Now humans state the Earth is round. Once this idea became a generally accepted truth it was not blasphemous to state this as fact.

Each person utters lies and false beliefs, and also truths, at various points in their day. The question a Seeker must ask is: how are those lies, beliefs and truths different from one another, and where inside your consciousness does each reside? From what place in the Seeker's consciousness has he or she uttered the statement that they perceive to be truth? The most comfortable behavior for many humans is to repeat what is programmed into them at an early age. A young child is a sponge, absorbing knowledge continually, and so can be easily manipulated by the world. Teach a child in school or church any belief and more than likely they will adhere to it and adopt it as their own, at least for awhile.

Seekers and Starseeds often feel different from other children because early on they will declare beliefs that do not mimic the beliefs held by the adults around them. A Starseed child might declare that they cannot buy into something simply because they were told it by an authority figure: parent, teacher, minister or police. The Seeker or Starseed has carried with them beliefs that do not integrate smoothly into the world around them, and this can be extremely challenging for a parent who merely wants to keep their child safe, or give their child what they feel is the best education. The parent thinks they know best, and the child appears rebellious. This is a clash of beliefs such as: "You will never be anything in this world without a good education," uttered by the parent, versus, "Freedom of thought is not going to be found in the stifling environment of a soul-deadening classroom," exclaimed by a Starseed child.

Now the problem begins: which of these two points of view are truth? Both? None? If each individual refuses to budge, and demands that their point of view be held as truth over the others, then conflict results. War is often ignited between two factions who hold opposing viewpoints. The largest moral dilemma a Seeker might face is speaking their personal truth in the face of opposition. If the story of Joan of Arc had taken place thousands of years ago, instead of merely hundreds, it is likely that it would be considered myth and legend. Yet, modern man is confronted with the truth of Joan with no convenient category in which to place her. She defies modern logic and truth. Giving her

Sainthood allowed humanity to dismiss the challenges of her existence. As a Saint no further explanation is necessary.

If Joan of Arc was a Seeker of truth, and closely in touch with her angelic guidance as she believed, and was documented, it seems reasonable to ask: Why was she captured? Why was she successful in such a massive endeavor as reclaiming the throne of France, and yet captured as she tried to take Paris? Did she fall from grace and lose her angelic support team? It is documented that Joan said, after she regained the throne for the French King, but then decided to continue to fight and take back Paris, that the voices who led her stopped talking to her altogether. Her angelic guidance stopped suddenly. She was alone. Why was that? Is it because her heavenly directive had been accomplished, and it was her human ego that needed to continue onward to Paris? When she tried to "take Paris" she was not working from her Higher-Self, but from her human ego. Perhaps she believed that she had to keep fighting, as she had become addicted to the battle and the glory associated with it. Surrender is always difficult for a warrior. But, is there not a lesson for all of us in her experience?

Joan was captured in Paris and put on trial; the rest, as they say, is history. Joan was declared guilty for a multitude of crimes that threatened the Powers that Be; not the least of which was dressing as a boy, instead of as a girl. Joan of Arc presents a challenge to many of our belief systems, for even the greatest skeptic finds it difficult to explain how a young, uneducated maid, managed to assemble and lead an army, and defeat the English troops. Most humans have enough trouble getting the family together for a BBQ to celebrate Aunt Jessie's birthday, or convincing a superior that their idea has merit. How did this uneducated maid, while on trial, resist the constant attacks on her mind, body and spirit? When she agreed at last to wear woman's clothing and rescind her statements to keep herself from burning at the stake she was betrayed and condemned to die in this most heinous manner despite her acquiescence. Why did she reclaim her truth and publicly declare her truth after the betrayal? Is it because that when one dishonors one's truth, one also dishonors one's soul? Joan reclaimed her soul when she reclaimed her truth. She died with honor.

Truth: A word bandied about but little understood. Why do so many martyrs die for their truth? Is the soul's truth sacred? Is it possible that when one denies one's truth one actually feels that one is selling one's soul to the devil? Is it possible that the denying of one's truth is the denying of one's sacred soul? Notice how empowered you feel when you stand tall in your truth, and how disempowered you feel when you lie. Practitioners of muscle testing will confirm that lies weaken, and truth strengthens the muscles. 88,000 lies by the time you are sixty is a lot of weakening.

When humans are denied access to their truth, or ostracized or bullied for it, they become depressed and angry. For example: homosexuals who must deny their most basic impulse to love, because of societal constraints, often feel depressed and angry. When the individual is restored to a life of honesty about who they are they regain something very important: their truth.

New Age beliefs have also been cemented into place by many Starseeds and Seekers longing once again to have peace and surety in a fundamentally unsure world. But, is comfort the ultimate goal for a Seeker? Is it not the job of knowledge to challenge the mind? Is knowledge a path to liberation? Is ignorance bliss? So, what does it mean to be a knowledge-keeper, gatherer or seeker? Are there different ways to gather knowledge? Can the heart and mind both be utilized? Nothing is so distressing to human beings than to have their well-worn beliefs challenged, or to have a comfort zone stirred up. The Seeker who seeks truth will find they feel quite alone at times as those around them would prefer the status quo to be left in place.

It is in religion that belief and truth most often become confused. Declaring one's beliefs as truth, by declaring one's Savior as the only, and superior to all others, creates a myriad of confusing thoughts in many humans. To ease the confusion fundamental principles are adopted and cemented in place; often devoid of the heart's interaction.

*Wisdom: the application of gathered knowledge through alignment of the heart's experiences, in an integrated expression of one's truth.*

Wisdom is not based on beliefs which might change and alter with the prevailing winds; instead wisdom is an accumulation of all one's life experiences throughout time and space.

The mind is easily manipulated and can be moved in numerous directions based on outside control systems and fear. The mind says, "I'm afraid if I don't cow-tow to my boss I'll lose my job." The heart says, "I am going to leave so I can find somewhere to be everyday that allows my truth to be expressed as valuable." Nobody likes to be treated like a robot, devoid of a soul. Being in an abusive marriage can deaden the heart and soul of a human being, until they feel they must strike out to set themselves free.

Maturity of the soul requires alignment of the heart, and mind, in a state of authentic truth. Breaking contracts with inauthentic truth is often painful, but necessary for one to reclaim one's Sacred Soul. Freedom is essential to reclaiming one's truth.

**EXERCISE TWELVE:** Declare your right to be sovereign and your intention to live as a Sacred Soul free to express your truth. Break any contracts that keep you out of alignment with your soul's purpose and in enslavement to anyone or anything. Honor the beliefs of yourself or others, but do not confuse those beliefs with truth. Fearlessly pursue the gathering of knowledge from all places, and integrate thoroughly the wisdom of the heart.

You might want to say something such as, "In God's name I break any and all contracts that I have made at any time that enslave me and keep me tethered to anyone or anything against my will. I am free to gather and integrate knowledge within me as I choose, and will not allow anyone to steal my Sacred Soul from me. I am a sovereign and free being, aligned with the truth of my heart."

Accept something as real that stretches your realm of possibility. Read a book that challenges your point of view. Talk to someone who believes something very different than you do and dialogue with him (peacefully) about your point of view.

# Chapter Thirteen

## *Manifesting Your Gifts:*
## *This And More Shall Ye Do*

So now you have stretched your mind, accessed your soul age, past lives, galactic past lives, and sacred tools. You've broken karmic bonds that held you back, recognized dark contracts and implants that control you, and freed your soul from those impediments. You reclaimed your soul, and have begun to see the truth of who you are unadorned by ego. You've met your fears; wrestled with greed and self-loathing. You've learned that you must love yourself fully to love others. You "know thyself," and now you are ready to begin the process of bringing all that awakening through you. The first thing you must do is recognize how much you have already begun to do that. Are you a Reiki Master? You've begun. Do you communicate with your Higher Self and the angelic realm? You've begun. Are you exercising your right to be different? You've begun. Do you accept that there are worlds of possibility beyond physical sight? You've already begun to manifest your gifts.

Before you rush ahead longing to manifest something else, appreciate what you have already manifested. Notice how different you are from what you were ten years ago. That is growth. Pat yourself on the back for taking the journey.

Next ask yourself, "What do I want to manifest?" and even more important, "Why?" Am I unhappy with my life so I think if I manifest _____ I will suddenly be happier? All the tools for happiness are available to you, and if you do not use the ones that have already been given why would your Higher Self give you more? So you can ignore those too? Gratitude means appreciating the gifts you have already been given, and using them to the fullest. Being like a greedy child at a birthday party who never stops to appreciate the gift they just received, but rushes head long into the next one frantically tearing off the paper, is not the way to manifest more gifts.

Once you make the pledge to be on the path as a Seeker your Higher Self is in charge of the ship. When you are ready to awaken a new gift you must do so with full co-operation of your Higher Self. Do you want to read your, or other people's past lives, and have access to the Akashic Records? You will not be given that ability until you step out of judgment. If you cannot see your (or another's) shadow without being in judgment of what you are perceiving, then you will not be given the information. Your soul must be mature enough to understand that all beings have a shadow, and it is not your job to judge another's journey through time and space. If you find yourself playing judge and jury every time you access your (or another person's) karmic records, then perhaps it is time to re-look at your own shadow. You cannot truly forgive others until you have truly forgiven yourself.

To be in one's power there are some rules that must be followed:

Never take personal energy away from somebody to weaken them: if the energy belongs there, leave it there. *(If a shaman tells you that their guides are telling them to disempower you, then something is wrong. Loving spirit guides want to empower you, and teach you to hold that power correctly.)*

Never put energy where it doesn't belong. This includes spells that are cast to energetically get someone, such as a curse, or get something, like a new car.

Never work on someone or something without its permission. *(Always ask their Higher Self for permission, and accept the outcome if the energy is not received by the intended recipient.)* Always do no harm. Work for the Highest Good of All Concerned.

What about taking out dark or evil energy you encounter in someone? Do you need permission? You cannot remove an evil or negative energy implant without the person's permission. You can try, but it won't work. Even if the person claims to want the entity out of them, if they are still emotionally attached to the entity it will not leave, or it will return. This is especially true with addictive behavior; the person may say they want the entity to be gone but unless they truly want to give up the bottle, or the drug, the entity will return. Many people receive comfort from these energies (they believe) because they have been with them for many lifetimes.

People also learn by wrestling with dark entities and energies, and if their Higher Self knows there is a lesson to be learned from the attachment it will not go away. You may think that getting the dark force out of the person is for their Highest Good, but don't blame yourself if the entity sticks around. Someone else's Highest Good may be feeling something quite different than you feel. For example, if someone was a dark witch in another life and spent many years casting curses on other people, you can be pretty sure their karmic payback will include many years of returned curses on them. If their karma is still necessary for them to learn something, you will not be able to alter the person's experiences. It is for the individual to clean up, and it is not your responsibility. Making them aware of their karma may assist them to move through it more quickly, and that is always helpful.

What about if you are psychically attacked by someone? Are you allowed to defend yourself? If someone has put a curse on you, or tried to harm you in any way, you are allowed to defend yourself; but you must send the energy that has been sent to you, back to them. You do not then retaliate with a curse of your own. That is revenge, and it creates karma. Mirror the energy that is being sent you back at the sender; this is within the laws of karma. What you sow you reap. What you send out, you receive back. You are allowed to defend yourself against attacks, and free yourself from curses, without adding extra retaliation to the event. If you do this you will be involved in witch and wizard wars and the ante will continually be upped. Return the energy and place energetic mirrors around you that face outward so that nothing can land on you, but is instead reflected back to the sender.

Working with subtle energy is tricky and not to be taken lightly. Be a conduit for Higher Energy Frequencies in alignment with Highest Good and Love and you can't go wrong.

Okay, that's simple, but I want to throw orbs. I want to move things telepathically. I want to teleport. I want to use crystals to magnify and manipulate energy. This is the realm of Merlin, and some of you are already doing these things. (Yes, you are.)

Manifesting these gifts spiritually requires that you are able to step off the lower Matrix and onto a higher Matrix. If you are vowing to work for the Highest Good, then the lower Matrix of doubt and density will block these gifts, but a higher vibrational state of consciousness releases the gifts.

The most common block to manifesting these gifts is the belief that you will be different. Being different brings with it all sorts of fears, and they must be released.

In many people's minds, being insane is only a small slip away from being different. Once you step enough off the familiar lower Matrix, and begin to alter your world, be prepared for everything to alter. Are you ready?

## EXERCISES FOR MANIFESTING GIFTS

1. This first exercise is simple and gentle, but will assist you to reconnect to the Earth in a loving and profound way. Too often, in these modern times, we rush from place to place, propelled by gasoline engines and surrounded by noise. As a result, we are disconnected from the natural world and the energy that the Earth supplies to us. The Earth's energy is essential to reawakening your abilities as a Co-Creator God. Without a connection to the Earth, you will not manifest your creation on this plane of existence, and that is what you are going to do. This work is about bringing the gift here, into third-dimensional reality, and lifting the vibration.

Find yourself a quiet place in nature. Noise drives away fairies and elves. Sit quietly and ask the fairies and elves to draw close. Then ask Archangel Ariel to join you (remember she is the angel of the nature realms). Fairies and elves communicate telepathically, so don't expect to hear them; more than likely you will feel their presence. Open the door to your heart to communicate with that realm. Return frequently to your sacred place and they will begin to trust you. Develop a relationship with the fairy realm.

2. While in your quiet and sacred place (indoors or out) begin to energize your hands. Hold them about five to seven inches away from each other in a cupped position. Feel an orb of energy in your hands. Manipulate it. Make it large and small. Bounce it in your palm. Throw it higher and catch it. Throw it from hand to hand. Change its color with your mind. Make it red, orange, yellow, green, blue and violet. Feel the frequency change as the color changes.

3. This exercise is where you will connect with Hamied the Angel of Miracles, as well as hone your Merlin gifts. It will assist you to reawaken your full potential as a creator. Find a quiet place where you will not be interrupted. Imagine yourself standing in the most serene, yet powerful environment you can envision. (It could the mountains, or the seashore, or a field, or by a stream.) Next, activate and align your seven on-body chakras, and then send energy down through your legs into the core of the Earth. Draw Earth energy into your body and anchor it into your solar plexus. Picture your solar plexus filled with the energy of the Earth.

Next you will send the energy out from the crown chakra. Place an $8^{th}$, $9^{th}$, $10^{th}$, $11^{th}$, $12^{th}$, $13^{th}$ and finally $14^{th}$ chakra out into the higher dimensions and connect the $14^{th}$ chakra to the God Source (**as shown in Chapter Eight**). Draw energy down from the God Source into your body and anchor it into the solar plexus. Allow these energies of heaven and Earth to balance within your body.

When you feel yourself anchored and empowered by these energies hold out your hands in front of you in a cupped, upward position. Envision a large white orb of light glowing in your palms. The energy you are holding is the energy of pure God creation; it is the energy of miracles. Feel it in your hands. Make it bigger and bigger as you define the edges of the orb. With your mind's eye, look into the orb, and place within it the thought, or idea you wish to manifest. Your mental, emotional and physical body must align with the desire, because they will kick-up if they are not in agreement. At this level you will find that your ego desires dissipate, and the higher consciousness prevails.

You cannot wish another's karma away; but you can pray, or choose to manifest for another's highest good, and then let go, and let God decide what the highest good is. Don't forget to manifest something for yourself; notice where your mental, emotional, or physical body is resistant. All three bodies must be in alignment to manifest on the third dimension. Practice this exercise often, until you feel comfortable with holding these energies of manifestation and miracles in your hands.

When you are done, close the orb up until it is the size of a baseball, cupped in your hands. Place your hands over the heart chakra, and seal the energy of God within your heart. Say, "I am in God, and God is within me."

4. Hold a glass of water in your hand and manipulate the molecules with your mind. Create love in the water. Create peace in the water. Create disturbance in the water. Notice the changes in the glass of water by sensing it.

5. Once you have made the energy in your hands, and mind, very real, and you can manipulate it, turn it into something: An apple, an orange, a grape. Close your eyes and use your mind to shift the energy into form. Play with this idea and notice how clearly your mind can project the thought of an object and how you will begin to feel that object in your palm. You might say, "Wow, it feels like an apple is sitting in my palm!"

6. Teleportation and Astral Projection. This must occur when the mind is holding very high vibration. It cannot be done from a state of fear or anger. Go deep into meditation and lift yourself into the $14^{th}$ chakra

as was described earlier. With your mind, move yourself to another location. Explore the location.

Teleportation will occur automatically when the vibration is correctly aligned. It cannot be pushed.

7. Crystals and the sacred tools. Select a crystal that speaks to you and listen to its message. Put it on your crown chakra or your third eye. It will tell you where it has been and what its purpose is. Incorporate the crystal in your spiritual work and use it in your healings if it is a healing crystal. Create a sacred tool from the crystal and utilize it as an ally in healing and journeys. Find the word (or words) that release the power of the crystal. Place the crystal on your third eye, and crown chakra, to amplify your astral journeys.

8. Connect to Mother Earth. Gaia is the name of Mother Earth; it is her angelic name. She is an angelic energy manifested in material form as the Earth. She has a soul, a heartbeat and she breathes in and out. She has wishes and desires, and she has needs and wants. Anchor your chakras deep into the Earth and listen to her heartbeat. Align your heart with hers. Now visit Agartha: the Inner Earth. Agartha exists in another dimension. It is the heart of the Earth in its Eden-like expression. Myths have told that native people have disappeared, and then reappeared in the fifth-dimensional Inner Earth, where peace reigns. It is more like Lyra, before it was attacked, because respect exists between all beings. They live harmoniously and hold open the vision for a perfected Earth. It has been written about as Shangri-La or Brigadoon. It is said to be fantasy, but it is another dimensional realm. To visit you must hold a high frequency; you cannot enter without unconditional love in your heart for *All* beings. The portals are guarded.

Open your heart to unconditional love and ask the Agarthans for entry. You may access their world through portals, which will reveal themselves to you when you are ready to enter, or you may enter through your lifted consciousness. Take a journey with your mind first. Then find an actual Agarthan portal on the Earth. This portal will feel safe, and protected. If the energy does not feel safe and held in a highly vibrational state, do not enter. Only step inside when invited to do so by loving beings. Another world waits. You may journey there only when invited.

## CONCLUSION

You have within you all you need to attain Mastery. No one can do it for you; and no one should. Honor the journeys of the Masters who have gone before you by seeing how long and (at times) arduous it was for them. Yours will be as well. Don't judge another person's journey. Take your own journey with self-love and respect for what you have, and will, undergo.

Be gentle with yourself on this journey. You will make what appear to be mistakes. They are opportunities to learn and grow. No one is perfect; and yet everyone is perfect in their imperfection. (*Let he who is without sin cast the first stone.*)

Do not exalt others above you. They are not. Do not denigrate others below you. They are not. See all beings as equal on a journey to self-mastery. They are.

It's all about the journey. There is no arrival. Enjoy the ride! You are a Seeker.